P9-DNE-593

Comma Sutra

Position Yourself *for* Success with Good Grammar

Laurie Rozakis, Ph.D.

Adams Media
Avon, Massachusetts

Published by
Adams Media, an F+W Publications Company
57 Littlefield Street, Avon, MA 02322. U.S.A.
www.adamsmedia.com

ISBN: 1-59337-279-5
Printed in the United States of America.

J I H G F E D C B A

Library of Congress Cataloging-in-Publication Data
Rozakis, Laurie.
Comma Sutra / Laurie Rozakis.
p. cm.
ISBN 1-59337-279-5
1. English language--Grammar--Handbooks manuals, etc.
2. English language--Usage--Handbooks manuals, etc. I. Title.
PE1112.R694 2004
428.2--dc22
2004022198

This publication is designed to provide accurate and authoritative information with regard to the subject matter covered. It is sold with the understanding that the publisher is not engaged in rendering legal, accounting, or other professional advice. If legal advice or other expert assistance is required, the services of a competent professional person should be sought.

—From a *Declaration of Principles* jointly adopted by a Committee of the American Bar Association and a Committee of Publishers and Associations

Many of the designations used by manufacturers and sellers to distinguish their products are claimed as trademarks. Where those designations appear in this book and Adams Media was aware of a trademark claim, the designations have been printed with initial capital letters.

This book is available at quantity discounts for bulk purchases. For information, please call 1-800-872-5627.

Acknowledgments

My deepest thanks to all the wonderful people who make me look so good:

Gary Krebs, director of publishing and a dear friend.

Danielle Chiotti, associate editor and every writer's dream editor.

Also thanks to Laura MacLaughlin, copy chief; Larry Shea, project manager; Paul Beatrice, cover artist; Daria Perreault, interior design; Heather Pagden, copyeditor.

Contents

Introduction

Like many Americans, you may be confused about what is the healthiest diet to follow. Consider the following facts:

1. Japanese eat very little fat and suffer fewer heart attacks than Americans.
2. Mexicans eat a lot of fat and suffer fewer heart attacks than Americans.
3. Africans drink very little red wine and suffer fewer heart attacks than Americans.
4. Italians drink excessive amounts of red wine and suffer fewer heart attacks than Americans.
5. Germans drink a lot of beer and eat lots of sausages and fats and suffer fewer heart attacks than Americans.

The conclusion? Go ahead and eat and drink what you like. Apparently, speaking English is what kills you.

If, after knowing all this, you still decide to run the risk of speaking and writing in English, you might as well take the trouble to do it correctly. Mastering any important skill can be scary and frustrating, and learning the basic rules of English grammar is no exception. But you've mastered many more difficult skills, and you know that using grammar with confidence can boost your personal and private life in a big way.

There are a lot of grammar books out there, but *Comma Sutra* is something new. It's a unique approach to the subject because it won't bore you with chapters and chapters of basics before getting to the meat of the matter—how

to write logical, complete, and graceful prose. To that end, *Comma Sutra* starts right in with sentences, incorporating the basics about parts of speech, punctuation, and capitalization. Then we move seamlessly into common grammar sinkholes, including agreement of subject and verb, pronoun and antecedent; double negatives, dangling and misplaced modifiers; and mixed metaphors. The book concludes with a section on style, progressing from diction to sentences, culminating in writing everyday documents.

To keep you laughing through your pain, I've used jokes, riddles, quips, and other funnies as grammar examples. If some of them don't make you laugh—or groan—don't blame me; I just work here. On the other hand, I take full responsibility for anything here that you find particularly witty or insightful.

By the end of this book, you'll be using English with confidence and skill. You'll be able to write great love letters and letters of complaint. You'll find it easier to get that promotion and that major hottie. So roll up your sleeves, kick back, and enjoy the ride.

PART ONE

Basic Training

Chapter 1

How We Got into THIS MESS

So for years you've been grousing, "This &%#*$ language is a mess. It doesn't follow the rules." Your significant other mutters back, "Stop carrying on. You can learn the rules if you want." Wait: You're both right. English grammar and usage *does* have a number of rules. Many of them are simple and very logical. Later in this book, I'll teach you all these rules and you'll find them a snap. You'll learn them easily.

But some of these rules do have exceptions. Check out the following famous one: How do you spell *fish*? *F-i-s-h* you say. Not so fast; it's also spelled *ghoti.* Here's how. Take the . . .

gh in *tough*

o in *women*

ti in *action*

and you get *ghoti* (or *fish*, as it's also spelled).

How is this possible? It's possible because English has forty elementary sounds but is written with twenty-six letters.

Psssst... between you and me, English has more quirks than the lady down the block who owns fifty-five cats. But relax: You'll discover that mastering the rules of English grammar and usage is much easier when you understand why the rules don't always follow the rules. So sit back, get a (German) beer, some (French) fries, and an order of (Chinese) takeout, and relax while I take you on a brief history of the English language. At the end of our trip around the world, you'll understand why English grammar is like the bad boys in the back row who just won't follow the rules.

Gimme Some Tongue

"Give me your tired, your poor, your huddled masses yearning to breathe free," Emma Lazarus wrote in a poem that was engraved on the base of the Statue of Liberty. She was probably thinking more of welcoming people than she was of welcoming words, but with one came the other.

English is the most democratic and unrestricted language that ever existed. We have welcomed into our language words from scores of other languages and dialects, near and far, ancient and modern. And when we can't find a word that we need, we just invent one to fit the bill. Here's how the story starts.

Land, Ho!

For ages, fair-haired hunky sailors from North Germany roamed the high seas at will. Not a terribly discerning lot, these so-called Angles, Saxons,

and Jutes aimed their beaked Viking ships at any country that promised booty. Around A.D. 449, the Anglo-Saxon mariners sailed across the North Sea and landed in a place they called "Britannia." They liked the countryside, so they decided to conquer the people and set up camp. That's your mini–*Masterpiece Theatre* version of how the Anglo-Saxons came to be the ancestors of English. It also explains why English is a Germanic language at heart.

SMARTY PANTS

The 100 most-often used words in English all come from the Anglo-Saxons—as do 83 of the next 100 words.

Ye Olde English

Today, we call the Anglo-Saxon language "Old English." It was a nice language and served the people's needs just fine, thank you very much, until 1066, when the Normans came to England with an army headed by William, Duke of Normandy. William and his soldiers spoke French. Harold Saxon, England's head honcho, tried to fight off William and his army, but failed. Since the Normans had no intention of learning Old English (the Norman language), they pressed their language on the masses. Hence, French became the official tongue. (Latin was used in church and school.) That's not to say that everyone suddenly stopped speaking Old English and started speaking French; actually, those stubborn peasants and their descendants kept right on chattering in Old English for another 300 years. In effect, William's victory added a new layer of language as well as a new government and some decent food.

Ye Olde Middle English

After the Normans, England was invaded over and over by cultures rather than warriors. As the English traded with their neighbors on the Continent, they acquired words as well as goods. It took about 300 years for Old English to become Middle English, and another 300 years for Middle English to become Modern English.

Around 1607, the Pilgrims, Puritans, and planters started hightailing it out of Europe, headed for our free and sunny shores. As early as 1621, Governor William Bradford and his fellow settlers in Plymouth Plantation were chatting up the Native Americans. Very quickly, American English became enriched with words from Native American dialects. Here are just a few words that we swiped from the Indians: *hickory, raccoon, possum, squash, powwow, chipmunk, moose, terrapin, quahog, hominy, pemmican, moccasin.* More than twenty-five U.S. states—from Massachusetts to the Dakotas—have Indian names.

And the words just keep on coming with wave after wave of immigration. Words travel to American English in different ways, from ships and steerage, on the *Concorde* and the *QE2.* Some of the richest sources of words are people from France, Spain, Italy, Germany, Poland, and Ireland. The Arab states, India, and Iran have also weighed in. Naturally, each major language layer brings subtle shifts in grammar and usage, too. Hey—no pain, no gain. You want a rich language, you gotta deal with some issues over the rules.

Duty Free: Imported Words

English never rejects a word because of its race, creed, or national origin. Let me prove it to you. Take this simple quiz to match each of the following words with its native language. Write the letter of the correct choice in the blank by the number.

Can I Borrow a Cup of Words?

	Word	Language of Origin
______	1. kimono	a. Arabic
______	2. tomato	b. West Indian
______	3. camel	c. Senegalese
______	4. algebra	d. Malayan
______	5. typhoon	e. Japanese
______	6. yam	f. French
______	7. mahogany	g. Mexican
______	8. ketchup	h. Yiddish
______	9. klutz	i. Hebrew
______	10. aspic	j. Chinese

Score Yourself:

Answers: 1-e; 2-g; 3-i; 4-a; 5-j; 6-c; 7-b; 8-d; 9-h; 10-f

SMARTY PANTS

According to *Ripley's Believe It or Not,* only 1 person in 100,000 can pronounce all of the following 10 words correctly. How well do you measure up? Give it a shot. Then check your pronunciation in a dictionary. Here are the words: *data, gratis, culinary, nuclear, gondola, version, impious, chic, Caribbean, Viking.*

Arguably, some of the most useful language contributions from our immigrants are curses. The Greeks gave us the always-apt, "May the red goats eat out your stomach lining and the white mice, too." Yiddish has contributed some especially effective curses. See who you can whammy with these examples (all translated, of course!):

May all your teeth fall out—but one should remain for a toothache.
May all your enemies move in with you.
May your sex life be as good as your credit.

What do we do if English doesn't have the word we need? We just make it up! Hey, Shakespeare made up more than 10 percent of the words that he used, and look where it got *him*. Besides, how do you think we came up with all those new computer terms like *byte*, *RAM*, and *ROM*?

The contributions of successive waves of immigrants have enriched our language immeasurably, but it also explains why grammar and usage stubbornly refuse to toe the line. After all, how can we have a standard set of rules when language changes faster than the shape of Michael Jackson's nose?

Mission Possible

Now you understand why it's not your fault: English *is* as screwy as you've always suspected. And now you know the reason: There aren't any grammar police rapping newcomers on the knuckles and admonishing, "Don't even be thinking of changing the language! No new words for you!" Just the opposite is true—English welcomes change and adapts accordingly.

But just because English can seem as stable as Jell-O doesn't let you off the hook. You realize that knowing how to use our glorious language is crucial. If you can't say it and write it clearly, you can't express yourself fully. People who know the difference between *lie* and *lay* or *who* and *whom* get a leg up on the ladder of success. Stick with me and you'll soon be on the top rung.

What exactly do you have to know? English has four standard areas of study. And here they are:

- Grammar
- Usage
- Punctuation and capitalization
- Style

Let's look at each one in detail.

Grammar

Grammar is one of those words like "IRS" and "root canal" that strikes fear in the heart of even the most stalwart. Not to worry: *Grammar* is just the rules of the language. Here's the technical definition: The set of rules that govern the way we speak and write is called the "grammar of the language."

Thus, grammar is just a systematic description of how the words fit together to make correct sentences. When Mrs. Schmendrick, your eleventh-grade English teacher, barked "Watch your grammar!" she meant "Use English properly." Each language has its own distinct grammar. Fortunately, English grammar is a lot easier than Chinese, Japanese, and Russian grammar. (See, there's always a silver lining.)

Grammars develop as spoken languages move into written versions. As the rules of a grammar become established, there's often a gap between what people say in casual conversation and what is considered correct in written forms. Here's an example:

Incorrect Grammar:
He says, "I don't know why you wear a bra. You ain't got nothing to put in it."
She says, "You wear pants, don't you?"

Correct Grammar:
He says, "I don't know why you wear a bra. You've got nothing to put in it."
She says, "You wear pants, don't you?"

We can argue the right to say "ain't" until the cows come home, but using incorrect grammar is like farting at a dinner party. Don't go there.

Get your feet wet with a few sample grammar rules:

- Use an adjective to describe a noun or a pronoun.
- Pronouns and antecedents (the words to which they refer) must agree, or match.
- Capitalize the names of languages, nationalities, and races.
- Use the nominative case to show the subject of a verb.
- Use only one negative word at a time to express a negative idea.
- Avoid shifting tenses in the middle of a sentence, paragraph, or essay.

Smarty Pants

One of the easiest ways to remember a word is to know its history. The word *grammar,* for example, comes from an Old French word that means "letter."

Usage

Usage is the way we actually use a language. In the best of all possible worlds, people would always use words according to the rules of English grammar. It just ain't so. Rather, people adapt their level of usage to their audience and purpose. This is not necessarily a bad thing, for reasons I'll explain throughout the book. In the meantime, here are some examples of common levels of usage.

Formal	Everyday	Nonstandard
follows all the grammar rules	follows most grammar rules	ignores most grammar rules
big words	common words	slang and not accepted words
no contractions	some contractions	many contractions
long sentences	midrange sentences	shorter sentences

Nonstandard English includes words and phrases that are not considered correct usage. Here is a list of words and phrases to avoid in speech and writing because they are considered nonstandard usage:

Nonstandard English	Standard Written English
irregardless	regardless
kind of a	kind of
off of	off
being that	since
had ought	ought
this here	this
hisself	himself

Nonstandard English	Standard Written English
the reason is because	the reason is since
like I told you	as I told you
that there	that

Come Again

A *gerund* is a form of a verb that acts as a noun. Gerunds always end in *–ing*. For example, "Kissing helps a person lose weight." Keep this in mind if you are ever called as a lifeline on *Who Wants to Be a Millionaire?*

Punctuation and Capitalization

Punctuation includes all those little marks that we use to separate words, groups of words, and sentences. Think of punctuation as the road signs on the highway of clear writing and speech. We especially need punctuation to tell us when to pause and when to stop when we read written English aloud.

Capitalization is the system we have for indicating the beginning of a sentence, a proper noun, a proper adjective, and other important words. Using the correct punctuation and capitalization is more than following the grammar rules—it enables your audience to understand your ideas more clearly.

Style

Style is an author's distinctive way of writing. Style is made up of elements such as:

- Word choice
- Sentence structure
- Tone
- Sentence length
- Punctuation
- Sentence variety
- Figures of speech

A writer may change his or her style for different kinds of writing and to suit different audiences. In poetry, for example, writers might use more imagery than they would use in prose (non-poetry).

Learn the Lingo

Everything worth knowing has its own special terms, and English is no exception. Some of these words sound a little salty, so you may be able to whisper them in your honey's ear if you run out of pillow talk. I can recommend "predicate nominative" and "parallel structure." Try, "You're such a hot predicate nominative," or "Wanna try some parallel structure when we finish watching the rinse cycle in the dishwasher?" Stay away from "dangling participle." Nothing should dangle in grammar or during those intimate moments, especially not your participles.

Here are ten grammatical terms and their definitions. Knowing them can improve your life more than a bit of a nip and tuck (and there's much less pain with grammar). That's why they're all explained in detail later in this book.

1. **Agreement**

Agreement means that sentence parts match in number (singular or plural).

2. **Case**

Case is the form of a noun or a pronoun that shows how it is used in a sentence. English has three cases: *nominative*, *objective*, and *possessive.*

3. **Dangling Modifier**

A *dangling modifier* is a word or phrase that describes something that has been left out of the sentence.

4. Fragment

A sentence *fragment* is a group of words that does not express a complete thought. Most times, a fragment is missing a subject, a verb, or both. Other times, a fragment may have a subject and a verb but still does not express a complete thought.

5. Parts of Speech

English words are classified into eight parts of speech according to their function in a sentence. The parts of speech are *adjectives*, *adverbs*, *conjunctions*, *interjections*, *nouns*, *prepositions*, *pronouns*, and *verbs*.

6. Phrases

Phrases are groups of words that function in a sentence as one part of speech. Phrases do not have subjects or verbs.

7. Sentences

A *sentence* is a group of words that expresses a complete thought. A sentence has two parts: a subject and a predicate. The subject includes the noun or pronoun that tells what the subject is. The predicate includes the verb that describes what the subject is doing.

8. Possession

Possession shows ownership.

9. Tense

In grammar, *tense* refers to time.

10. Transitions

Transitions are words that connect ideas and show how they are linked.

Chapter 2

Assume the Position: NOUNS, PRONOUNS, VERBS

A little girl asks her mother, "Can I go outside and play with the boys?"

Her mother replies, "No, you can't play with the boys. They're too rough."

The little girl replies, "If I find a smooth one, can I play with him?"

In this chapter, I'll introduce you to all eight parts of speech. Then we'll cover nouns, pronouns, and verbs in detail. I promise that it will all go down smoothly.

Behind the Eight Ball

In an effort to make English more user-friendly, some dead grammar person divided our words into eight parts of speech, according to their function in a sentence. Here are the eight parts of speech in a simple cheat sheet (feel free to clip and save, my Cupcake).

The Eight Parts of Speech

nouns . . . . .name people, places, or things
verbs . . . . .name an action or a state of being
pronouns. . . . . .take the place of a noun
adjectives . . . . .describe nouns and pronouns
adverbs . . . . .describe verbs, adjectives, or other adverbs
conjunctions . . . . .connect words or groups of words
prepositions. . . . . .link a noun or pronoun to another word
interjections. . . . . .show strong emotion

This reads better than it plays, of course, because some words can be more than one part of speech, depending on how they are used in a sentence. Let's get this bit of nastiness out of the way so we can get to the fun.

I present for your inspection Exhibit A. Each of the following sentences shows the same word used as two different parts of speech. I've labeled each word pair.

1. The farm was used to <u>produce</u> <u>produce</u>.
   verb noun

2. A <u>bass</u> was painted on the head of the <u>bass</u> drum.
   noun adjective

3. The dump was so full that it had to <u>refuse</u> more <u>refuse</u>.
   verb noun

4. At the <u>present</u> time, we'll give them the <u>present</u>.
   adjective noun

5. The soldier decided to <u>desert</u> in the <u>desert</u>.
   verb noun

But you have smart brains, so you realize that it's not as bad as it looks at first blush. For one thing, many of these words are pronounced differently, so you can easily tell them apart. Second, if you're into pain, you'll be doing the whip-and-chain thing, not writing silly sentences like these.

Now that you've gotten smacked with the bad news, here's the good news: The parts of speech are logical and easy to use. Really. Let's start with the basics: nouns, verbs, and pronouns.

Show and Tell

Nouns and verbs are the meat and potatoes of English grammar: When you have one of each, you've got a sentence. When you've got a sentence, you can express yourself in a full and logical unit of thought.

Nouns: What's in a Name?

William Shakespeare asked, "What's in a name? A rose by any other name would smell as sweet." Keep names in mind and you have nouns licked. A *noun* is a word that names a person, place, or thing. There are three main types of nouns: *common nouns*, *proper nouns*, and *compound nouns*. Let's look at each one in detail.

Common Nouns

Common nouns name a type of person, place, or thing. They're the white bread of nouns, as popular as your buddy with a platinum card with no balance. Common nouns are helpful, too, as useful as a tube of raw cookie dough at 2:00 A.M. after you've had a really bad, terrible, awful day. After all, you

can't write a sentence without a noun, and most of the time the nouns you use will be the common garden-variety ones, like these . . .

- woman, female, lady, adult
- town, city, village, municipality
- dog, puppy, canine, hound, pooch

Proper Nouns

Proper nouns name a specific person, place, or thing. You can easily distinguish between common nouns and proper nouns because proper nouns ALWAYS start with a capital letter. Common nouns only start with a capital letter if they're the first word in a sentence. They're not getting any special treatment here; the first word of every sentence is capitalized, no matter what part of speech it happens to be. Here are some proper nouns:

- Anna Nicole Smith, Britney Spears, J.Lo, Dame Edna
- Las Vegas, Nevada; Des Moines, Iowa; Portland, Maine; Intercourse, Pennsylvania (It is a real town in Pennsylvania, you pervert.)
- Lassie, Rin Tin Tin, Snoopy, Odie, Checkers

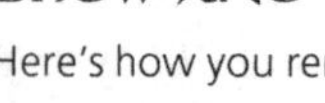

Show and Tell

Here's how you remember that a compound noun is made of two or more words: A compound is made up of two or more parts. Compound interest is interest on the principal and the interest; a compound eye has different parts.

Compound Nouns

Compound nouns are two or more nouns that work together as one word. A compound noun can be two individual words, words joined by a hyphen, or two words combined. No matter how they're connected, if they're treated as one unit, they're considered a compound noun. Here are some examples:

- outhouse, outpost, outside, outlaw
- out-of-date, out-of-doors
- eye shadow, eye drops, eye socket

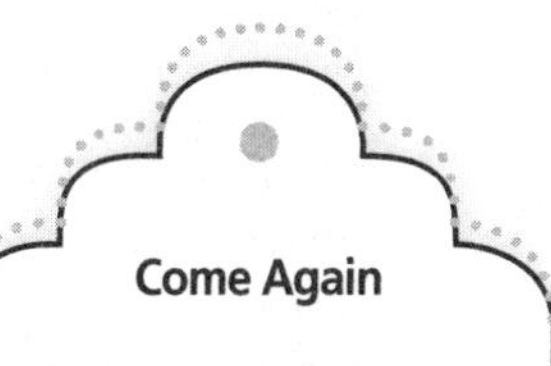

Come Again

There's also a fourth type of noun: a *collective noun*. These nouns play well with others: They name a group of people or things. Here are some collective nouns: *team, crew, corps, company, squad.*

Drive It On Home

Circle the nouns in the following passage. If you're feeling especially frisky, label each type of noun. (But not to worry; as long as you can recognize a garden-variety noun, you're home free.)

A woman is driving in Arizona when she comes upon a Navajo woman hitchhiking. Because the trip has been long and boring, the driver stops the car and picks up the Navajo woman. During their small talk, the Navajo woman glances surreptitiously at a brown bag on the front seat between them.

"If you're wondering what's in the bag," the driver says, "It's a bottle of wine. I got it for my husband."

The Navajo woman says, "Good trade."

Answers:

woman, Arizona, woman, trip, driver, car, woman, talk, woman, bag, seat, bag, driver, bottle, wine, husband, woman, trade

Possessive Nouns

Just like in real life, when it comes to English, *possession* means ownership. Only nouns can show possession because only people, places, or things can own anything. Thus, you never show possession with a verb, adjective, adverb, and so on. Only nouns. Ever.

English has two ways to show possession:

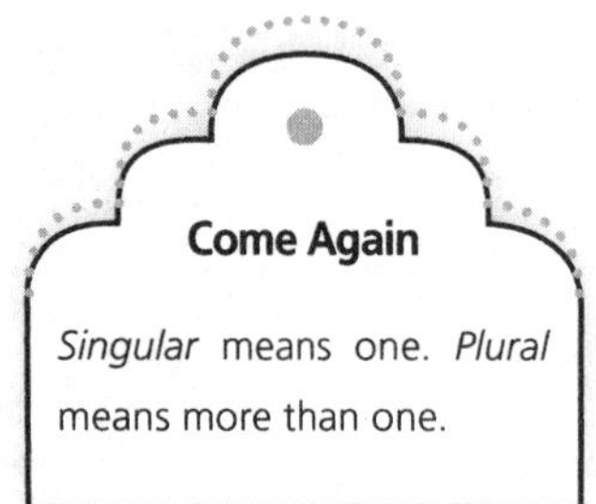

Way #1: The nose ring and bifocals of Granny *or* The nose ring and bifocals that belong to Granny

Way #2: Granny's nose ring and bifocals

Clearly, Way #2 is way better because it is more direct and less cumbersome. All you have to do is use that little apostrophe, that comma in the air. It looks like this: **'** . Here are a few examples:

The book of Pasqual........becomes ...... Pasqual's book
The room of the women.....becomes ...... the women's room
The tattoos of the girls .....becomes ...... the girls' tattoos

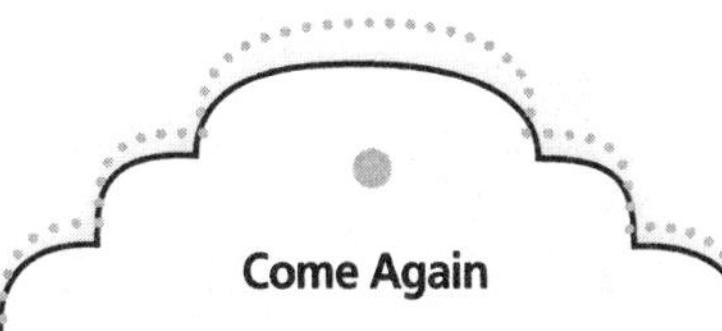

Come Again

Here are the rules to create possessive nouns using apostrophes:

1. Add an apostrophe and an *s* to singular nouns.

frog . . . . frog's tongue
William Shatner . . . William Shatner's singing
Girl Scout . . . . Girl Scout's cookies

2. Add an apostrophe after the *s* with plural nouns ending in *s*.

frogs . . . . frogs' tongues
Trekkies . . . . Trekkies' songs
Girl Scouts . . . . Girl Scouts' cookies

3. Add an apostrophe and an *s* with plural nouns not ending in *s*.

men . . . . men's socks
mice . . . . mice's holes
fish . . . . fish's bubbles

Drive It On Home

Revise the underlined part of the following jokes to have fewer words by using the possessive form of the noun.

1. What is a favorite soap opera of a bee? *"Days of Our Hives"*

   ____

   ____

2. Where do you find the biggest spider in the world? *In the World Wide Web*

   ____

   ____

3. Why did the Dalmatian go to the store of the cleaner? *His coat had spots all over it.*

   ____

   ____

4. What is a favorite ballet of a squirrel? *"The Nutcracker"*

   ____

   ____

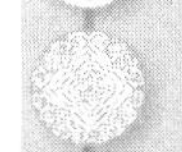

5. What is the favorite game show of a fish? *"Name That Tuna"*

____

6. What is the favorite song of Tarzan? *"Jungle Bells"*

____

7. Why was the stadium of the Yankees so hot after the game? *All the fans had left.*

____

8. What is the favorite TV show of a potato? *"MASH"*

____

9. Why was the head of the scientist wet? *He had a brainstorm.*

____

10. Where is the temple of King Solomon? *On the side of his head*

____

Answers:

1. bee's favorite soap opera
2. world's biggest spider
3. cleaner's
4. squirrel's favorite ballet
5. fish's favorite game show
6. Tarzan's favorite song
7. Yankees' stadium
8. potato's favorite TV show
9. scientist's head
10. King Solomon's temple

Pronouns

Think of pronouns as nouns in the Witness Protection Program. Pronouns are words used in place of a noun or another pronoun. Naturally, pronouns come in different flavors. Here are a half dozen different types: *personal pronouns, possessive pronouns, relative pronouns, demonstrative pronouns, interrogative pronouns, indefinite pronouns.*

Personal Pronouns

All pronouns take the place of a noun. *Personal pronouns* refer to a specific person, place, object, or thing. Study this chart:

Personal Pronouns

	Singular Pronouns	**Plural Pronouns**
first person	I, me, mine, my	we, us, our, ours
second person	you, your, yours	you, your, yours
third person	he, him, his, she, her, hers, it	they, them, their, theirs, its

Here are some examples:

Q: How many honest, intelligent, caring <u>men</u> (noun) in the world does it take to do the dishes?

A: Both of <u>them.</u> (pronoun)

In the second sentence, the pronoun *them* takes the place of the noun *men.*

A crocodile cannot stick out its tongue.

noun pronoun

The pronoun *its* takes the place of the noun *crocodile.*

Don't confuse plural pronouns with contractions. You know that a *pronoun* is a word that takes the place of a noun. A *contraction* is a word or phrase that has been shortened by leaving out one or more letters. Contractions use apostrophes to show where a letter or letters have been left out. Pronouns NEVER use apostrophes. Study the following chart:

Pronouns	**Contractions**
its	it's
your	you're
there, their	they're
whose	who's

Possessive Pronouns

Possessive pronouns show ownership. The possessive pronouns are *my, your, yours, his, her, hers, its, our, ours, their, theirs, whose.* Notice that they do not use apostrophes.

Relative Pronouns

Relative pronouns begin a subordinate clause (a group of words that cannot stand alone in a sentence). There are five relative pronouns:

- that
- those

- which
- who
- whom

Demonstrative Pronouns

Demonstrative pronouns indicate a specific person, place, or thing. Happily, there are only four demonstrative pronouns:

- this
- that
- these
- those

Interrogative Pronouns

Interrogative pronouns are used to ask questions. There are five of these:

- what
- which
- who
- whom
- whose

Show and Tell

No, you're not crazy: Some pronouns can function in two or more capacities. For example, *who* and *whom* are relative pronouns as well as interrogative pronouns, depending on how they are used.

Indefinite Pronouns

Indefinite pronouns refer to people, places, objects, or things without specifying which ones. Here are some common indefinite pronouns:

all	another	any	anyone
both	each	everybody	everyone
everything	few	many	more
most	nobody	none	nothing
others	several	some	something

Come Again

An *antecedent* is the noun (or group of words acting as a noun) for which the pronoun stands. Here is an example:

Because of _its_ climate, _hell_ is not my favorite city.

pronoun antecedent

Drive It On Home

Circle the pronouns in this story:

A ninety-year-old man bragged to his doctor, "I have never felt better. I have an eighteen-year-old bride who is pregnant with my child. What do you think of that?"

The doctor thought about this for a minute and then said, "I have an elderly friend who is a hunter and never misses a season. One day he was going out to hunt in a bit of a hurry, and he accidentally picked up his umbrella instead of his rifle. When he got to the creek, he saw a beaver sitting

beside the stream. He raised his umbrella and went, "'Bang! Bang!' And the beaver fell down dead. What do you think of that?"

The ninety-year-old said, "I would say someone else shot that beaver."

The doctor replied, "My point exactly."

Answers:

his, I, I, who, my, you, that, I, who, he, he, his, his, he, he, He, his, What, you, that, I, someone, My

Verbs

Verbs are words that name an action or describe a state of being. Verbs are often small critters but they pack a big wallop because they are the predicate half of a sentence.

Remember that every sentence must have two parts: a *subject* and a *predicate.*

- A *subject* is a noun or a pronoun. It tells who does the action.
- A *predicate* is a verb. It tells what action is done.

Here are the three types of verbs: *action verbs, linking verbs,* and *helping verbs.* Let's examine them now.

Action Verbs

Action verbs do just what you would expect: They describe an action. The verb's action can be something you can see (such as "sleep," "eat," "drink") or something that takes place in your mind (such as "imagine," "discover," "memorize"). The action verbs are underlined in the following sentences:

> "I am a marvelous housekeeper. Every time I leave a man I keep his house." (Zsa Zsa Gabor)

> "I refuse to think of them as chin hairs. I think of them as stray eyebrows." (Janette Barber)

Linking Verbs

Linking verbs are also a snap because their name fits their function: They link the subject and the predicate. Thus, they connect the noun or pronoun at the beginning of the sentence with a word near the end.

Remember the famous quote from *Hamlet* and you'll be able to identify most linking verbs: "To be or not to be." That's *be*cause most linking verbs are a form of the verb *to be.* Here are the most common incarnations of *to be*:

- am, are, is, was, were
- am being, are being, is being, was being, were being
- can be, could be, may be, might be, must be, shall be, should be, will be, would be
- have been, has been, had been, could have been, may have been, might have been, must have been, shall have been, should have been

Naturally, things can't be quite that easy, so we have a handful of linking verbs that aren't forms of *to be.* They're easy to remember, however, because they tend to deal with the senses:

appear	look	sound
become	remain	stay
feel	seem	taste
grow	smell	turn

Linking verbs are used a great deal. Following are two examples. The linking verbs are underlined in each sentence.

Invaders from Mars remains the world's scariest movie.
"Behind every successful man is a surprised woman." (Maryon Pearson)

Many linking verbs can also be used as action verbs. For example:

- *Linking:* The cat *looked* hungry.
- *Action:* I *looked* for the cat under the sofa.

Helping Verbs

Helping verbs are verbs that can be added to another verb to make the meaning clearer. When a helping verb is added to another verb, a *verb phrase* is created. Helping verbs include any form of *to be.* Here are some examples:

- do, did, does
- have, has, had
- shall, should, will, would
- can, could, may, might, must

Drive It On Home

You know the drill: Circle the verbs or verb phrases in each sentence.

1. The phrase "working mother" is redundant.
2. Every time I close the door, reality comes in through the windows.
3. "I am not offended by all the dumb blond jokes because I know I am not dumb . . . and I am not a blond." (Dolly Parton)
4. "The hardest years in life are those between ten and seventy." (Helen Hayes, at age seventy-eight)
5. A male gynecologist is like an auto mechanic who never owned a car.

Answers:

1. is
2. close, comes
3. am not offended, know, am, am
4. are
5. is, owned

Chapter 3

Spice Up Your Life: ADD MODIFIERS

Here are five tips I've heard for how a woman can spice up her life:

1. It is important that a man helps you around the house and has a job.
2. It is important that a man makes you laugh.
3. It is important that you find a man you can count on and who doesn't lie to you.
4. It is important that a man loves you and spoils you.
5. It is important that these four men don't know each other.

I have an easier way to spice up your life: Add some adjectives and adverbs. It's far simpler than finding four different fellas (or whatever floats your boat, boys and girls). So let's start all that jazz.

Adjectives

Adjectives are words used to describe a noun or pronoun. By so doing, adjectives give the noun or pronoun a more precise and specific meaning. For example:

Noun without an adjective	Jerk!
Noun with an adjective	Stupid (adjective) jerk!

See how much more effective adjectives make your speech and writing? Adding that adjective "stupid" makes all the difference in effectiveness. (Other adjectives work equally well in this situation, such as *insipid, boring, tedious, asinine, dimwitted,* and *cheap.*)

The adjective can come before or after the noun or pronoun it describes. Here are some examples:

Before the noun:

Grandpa Sheldon wore an ankle (adjective) bracelet (noun) with his corn (adjective) pads (noun).

After the noun:

The elephant (noun), sick (adjective) with mumps, amused himself with crossword puzzles.

Before the pronoun:

Sick (adjective) in bed, she (pronoun) was in no state to play footsie with Dumbo.

After the pronoun:

She was sick for a week.
pronoun adjective

Adjectives would do a good job in a police interrogation because they respond well to questions. Here are the four questions that make these words different from all others:

How to Identify Adjectives

Question	Examples
What kind?	long tongue
How much?	fifty dollars
Which one?	that night
How many?	several times

SMARTY PANTS

In grammar speak, the "describing" that adjectives and adverbs do is called "modifying." Thus, a grammar hottie would say, "Gee, check out how that adjective modifies that noun."

There are several different types of adjectives. Let's consider three of them: *articles, compound adjectives, proper adjectives.* To be fair to these useful words, we'll discuss them in alphabetical order.

Articles

This one is a walk in the park because there are only three articles: *a, an, the. A* and *an* are called "indefinite articles" because they refer to general

things. Use *a* before nouns that begin with a consonant sound; use *an* before nouns that begin with a vowel sound. Focus on the word "sound": The noun can begin with a vowel but if the vowel has a consonant sound, the article is *a*, not *an*. Articles can also be used before adjectives and adverbs, as in "an awfully ugly date," for example. Here are some other examples:

Using Articles Correctly

With Consonant Sounds	With Vowel Sounds
a football	an onion
a history book	an honest mistake
a one-horse town	an only child
a union	an ugly date

The is called a "definite article" because it refers to a specific thing. For instance:

the shotgun formation — the rubber chicken

Drive It On Home

Circle the correct article in each of these sentences.

You live in Florida when . . .

1. You eat dinner at 3:15 in (a, an, the) afternoon.
2. All purchases include (a, an, the) coupon of some kind—even houses and cars.
3. Everyone can recommend (a, an, the) excellent dermatologist.
4. Road construction never ends anywhere in (a, an, the) state.
5. There are only GIANT doctors in Florida: Everyone's doctor is "(a, an, the) Biggest" in her field.

You live in the Midwest when . . .

6. You've never met any celebrities, but (a, an, the) mayor knows your name.
7. Your idea of (a, an, the) traffic jam is ten cars waiting to pass (a, an, the) tractor.
8. You have switched from "heat" to "AC" on (a, an, the) same day.
9. You end sentences with (a, an, the) preposition, such as "Where's my coat at?"
10. When asked how your trip was to (a, an, the) exotic place, you say, "It was different!"

Answers:

1. the	2. a	3. an	4. the	5. the
6. the	7. a, a	8. the	9. a	10. an

Compound Adjectives

Like compound nouns, compound adjectives are made up of two words. For instance:

<u>all-American</u> <u>cowboy</u>
adjective noun

<u>far-off</u> <u>land</u>
adjective noun

Size *Does* Matter

Allow me to climb onto my soapbox for a moment, my friends. After all, you like me, you really like me! Here's my rant: When you write and speak, use the exact word you want, not some evasive, sneaky, Tricky Dick substitute. For example, if you have a secondhand car, call it a "used car," not a "preowned car." If you're getting your body sliced and diced, call it "surgery," not a "procedure." That way, not only are you using language honestly and responsibly, but people will know what you're talking about. We'll go into this in detail in Chapter 13. Thank you for letting me get this off my chest.

Proper Adjectives

Some proper adjectives are simply proper nouns used as adjectives. Others are adjectives formed from a proper noun. No matter what their birth, all proper adjectives are capitalized. Here are some examples:

- French bread, Spanish rice, Greek olives, Polish sausage, German beer
- African art, Latin music, Greek architecture, Dutch dikes
- Native American names, Jeffersonian democracy, Roman legions

When proper nouns are used as adjectives, their form may or may not remain the same, as you noticed in the previous list. To make your life as easy as pie, the following chart reinforces how proper nouns transform into proper adjectives.

ABRACADABRA: Proper Nouns Used as Proper Adjectives

Proper Nouns	Proper Adjectives
California	California grapes
February	February snowstorm
Clinton	Clinton administration
Shakespeare	Shakespearean comedies

Show and Tell

When you see the word "proper," as in *proper noun* and *proper adjective,* you know the word has to be capitalized—no matter where it appears in a sentence.

Drive It On Home

Circle the adjective or adjectives in each of the following items. Some are proper adjectives, some are compound adjectives, and some are just regular old garden-variety adjectives.

1. Superman came to Earth from a far-off planet.
2. Superman is all-powerful, except maybe for his issues with kryptonite.
3. You live in Alaska when . . . You only have four spices: salt, pepper, ketchup, and Tabasco.
4. You live in Alaska when . . . You have many recipes for moose.
5. You live in Alaska when . . . Halloween costumes fit over parkas.
6. You live in Alaska when . . . The four seasons are: winter, still winter, almost winter, and construction.
7. April showers make messes in my nice garden.
8. You can keep May flowers.
9. What is the point of brick wallpaper?
10. How come we never hear any father-in-law jokes?
11. He had a bad case of hard-shelled crabs.
12. Age is the outrageous price paid for maturity.

Answers:

1. far-off
2. all-powerful
3. four
4. many
5. Halloween
6. four, still, almost
7. April, nice
8. May
9. brick
10. father-in-law
11. bad, hard-shelled
12. outrageous

Recycling Words

Remember back in the dawn of time (as in Chapter 2), I mentioned that some words can function as more than one part of speech? Whether you remember it or not, work with me here. Gee, *someone* has to.

Nouns Used as Adjectives

Sure enough, common nouns can also function as adjectives. They do so a lot of the time, too. This may seem like a pain in the arse, but this flexibility with language is one of the features that gives English its great strength. If we don't have the word we need, we simply repurpose a word that we already have. The following chart has some examples of nouns used as adjectives.

Word as a Noun	Word as an Adjective
piano	piano music
afternoon	afternoon nap
fruit	fruit drink
name	name brands

To determine whether a noun is functioning in a sentence as an adjective, see if it answers the questions "What kind?" or "Which one?"

But wait! There's more!

Pronouns Used as Adjectives

Pronouns can also function as adjectives. The following chart has some examples.

Word as a Pronoun	Word as an Adjective
her	her umbrella
that	that book
which	which movie
what	what earrings

Many of the indefinite pronouns can also be used as adjectives. So many indefinite pronouns are used as adjectives that we even have a name for them: *indefinite adjectives.* I've always liked that one because it makes so much sense: Swipe the "indefinite" from *indefinite pronouns* and add it to the word "adjective." Here are some examples of indefinite adjectives:

adjective	noun
another	day
many	coworkers
all	fools
more	work
some	aggravation
few	victories

To determine whether a pronoun is functioning in a sentence as an adjective, see if it answers the question "Which one?"

Drive It On Home

Circle the adjectives in these sentences. The number in ( ) tells you how many to find in each sentence.

The Rules for Women as Defined by Men:

1. Sunday sports: They are like the full moon or the tides. Let it be. (4)
2. A headache that lasts for seventeen months is a problem. See a doctor. (4)
3. Anything we said last night is inadmissible in an argument. In fact, all comments become null and void after seven days. (5)
4. If you won't dress like the Victoria's Secret girls, don't expect us to act like the soap opera guys. (4)
5. Peach is a fruit, not a color. (2)
6. Don't ask us what we're thinking, unless you are prepared to discuss such topics as armchair baseball or monster trucks. (3)
7. You have enough clothes. (1)
8. Learn to work the toilet seat. (1)
9. Ask for what you want. Subtle hints do not work. (1)
10. "Yes" and "no" are acceptable answers to every question. (2)

Answers:

1. Sunday, the, full, the
2. A, seventeen, a, a
3. last, inadmissible, an, all, seven
4. the, Victoria's Secret, the, soap opera
5. a, a
6. such, armchair, monster
7. enough
8. toilet
9. Subtle
10. acceptable, every

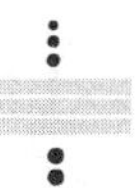

Show and Tell 

Use vivid adjectives to make your writing and speech more specific and descriptive.

Blah sentence lacking vivid adjectives:	A middle-aged fashion mistake is a *small* ring and a *stomach* scar.
Zippy sentence with vivid adjectives:	A middle-aged fashion mistake is a *bellybutton* ring and a *gallbladder* scar.

Adverbs

Adverbs are words used to describe a verb, an adjective, or another adverb. By so doing, adverbs give the verb, adjective, or other adverb a more precise and specific meaning. For example:

Verb without an adverb	spent
Verb with an adverb	spent a lot (adverb)
Adjective without an adverb	broke
Adjective with an adverb	very (adverb) broke
Adjective without an adverb	solvent
Adjective with adverbs	only (adverb) just (adverb) solvent

Adverbs can come before or after the verb they describe. Here are some examples:

Before the verb: Do you completely understand the situation?
adverb verb

After the verb: Our neighbors are moving away.
verb adverb

Adverbs come before the adjectives they describe. Here are some examples:

Before the adjective:
We are very glad that Mr. and Mrs. Dullard have moved.
adverb adjective

Before the adjective:
The new neighbors look extremely pale and don't go out during the day.
adverb adjective

Also, adverbs come before any adverbs they describe. Here are some examples:

Before the adverb: Our fears are almost completely gone.
adverb adverb

Before the adverb: Please move your neck farther forward.
adverb adverb

Like adjectives, adverbs would do well being grilled by your mother at 2:00 A.M. because they answer questions. Here are the four questions that make these words different from all others:

How to Identify Adverbs

Question	Examples
Where?	move aside
When?	arrived yesterday
In what manner?	talked smoothly
To what extent?	partly understand

A Leopard and His Stripes

Many adverbs end in *–ly*. That's because most adverbs are formed by adding *–ly* to an adjective. The following chart shows some examples of this clever system.

Making Adjectives into Adverbs

Adjectives	Adverbs
gentle	gently
bright	brightly
slow	slowly
poor	poorly

Naturally, we can't leave well enough alone. A whole lot of adverbs are not formed from adjectives. They don't end in *–ly*. This means you can't always say, "Oh, that cute word has to be an adverb because it ends in *–ly*." Rather, you must always see how the word functions in the sentence. Following are some examples of adverbs that you can depend on to follow the rule and those that insist on being different.

Adverbs and Rear Action

Adverbs That End in *–ly*	Adverbs That Don't End in *–ly*
brightly	very
slowly	never
quickly	seldom
easily	always
nicely	somewhat
extremely	just
amazingly	more
fairly	almost

Drive It On Home

Circle the adverb or adverbs in each of these sentences.

1. Julia massaged his buttocks briskly.
2. Yesterday she forgot to buy massage oil.
3. She always follows the directions carefully.
4. Nonetheless, the client looked extremely upset after the massage.
5. He ran surprisingly quickly from the massage parlor.
6. The dog moved somewhat closer to the squirrel.
7. The squirrel just barely got out of the way in time.
8. The dog barked confidently about his adventure.
9. His confidence was partially justified.
10. This adventure will end abruptly.

Answers:

1. briskly
2. Yesterday
3. always, carefully
4. Nonetheless, extremely
5. surprisingly, quickly
6. somewhat, closer
7. just, barely, out
8. confidently
9. partially
10. abruptly

Who's Who?

Here are some of the questions that drive us 'round the bend: Is that a pair of stylish footwear or a medieval torture device? Is that lump on the steam table a carb or a protein? Is that person trying to pick up a man or a woman? Worst of all, is that word an adjective or an adverb?

I can't help you with the first three issues (other than to say, "If the shoe fits, don't buy it."). Fortunately, I *can* help you with the problem of distinguishing between adjectives and adverbs.

Here's another Clip 'n' Save chart to post on your dashboard or have tattooed on your stomach.

Why Can't an Adjective Be More Like an Adverb?

Adjectives	Adverbs
describe nouns	describe verbs
describe pronouns	describe adverbs
	describe adjectives

Drive It On Home

Guess the identity of the underlined word in each of the following sentences by circling either "adjective" or "adverb."

A contest in the *Washington Post* invites readers to take any word from the dictionary, alter it by adding, removing, or changing one letter, and then come up with a new definition. Here are some of the winning entries:

1. Hipatitis: terminal coolness

   adjective or adverb

2. Osteopornosis: a _degenerate_ disease
   adjective or adverb

3. Glibido: _all_ talk and no action
   adjective or adverb

4. Dopeler effect: the tendency of stupid ideas to seem smarter when they come at you _rapidly_
   adjective or adverb

5. Inoculatte: to take coffee intravenously when you are running _very_ late
   adjective or adverb

6. Bozone: the substance surrounding a stupid person that stops _bright_ ideas from penetrating
   adjective or adverb

7. The Bozone layer, unfortunately, shows little sign of breaking _down_ in the near future.
   adjective or adverb

8. Cashtration: the act of buying a house, which renders the subject financially impotent for an _indefinite_ period
   adjective or adverb

9. Karmageddon: it's like when someone is sending off these _really_ bad vibes, right?
   adjective or adverb

10. And then, like, the Earth explodes and it's, like, a _serious_ bummer.
    adjective or adverb

Answers:

1. adjective. . . . . . . describes the noun "coolness"
2. adjective. . . . . . . describes the noun "disease"
3. adverb . . . . describes the verb "talk"
4. adverb . . . . describes the verb "come"
5. adverb . . . . describes the adverb "late"
6. adjective. . . . . . . describes the noun "ideas"
7. adverb . . . . describes the verb "breaking"
8. adjective. . . . . . . describes the noun "period"
9. adverb . . . . describes the adjective "bad"
10. adjective. . . . . . . describes the noun "bummer"

Chapter 4

Bondage 101: CONJUNCTIONS

Duct tape connects the objects in our world, and it does a fine job of it, too. However, duct tape gets a little cumbersome when you have to stick it all over your sentences to hold the words together. That's why *conjunctions* were invented. They link together words and groups of words. They're as good as duct tape and a whole lot cheaper, too.

Best of all, conjunctions show the relationship between words and ideas. Can duct tape do that? Heck, no!

There are three kinds of conjunctions: *coordinating conjunctions*, *subordinating conjunctions*, and *correlative conjunctions*. In this chapter, you'll meet the conjunction family and discover why these little words pack such a wallop. You'll also find out how to use conjunctions to link individual words and groups of words. This is the basis for writing logical, cohesive, and effective sentences.

Coordinating Conjunctions

Coordinating conjunctions are used to link related words or related groups of words. There are only seven coordinating conjunctions:

- and
- but
- for
- nor
- or
- so
- yet

You can remember the seven coordinating conjunctions if you put them in this silly word: *BANFOYS: but, and, nor, for, or, yet, so.*

Using Coordinating Conjunctions

Coordinating conjunctions are used to link words and groups of words. First, we'll see how coordinating conjunctions join individual words, including nouns, verbs, adjectives, and prepositional phrases. In the following examples, the conjunctions are in bold type.

Coordinating conjunctions used to link nouns:

The verb "cleave" is the only English word with two synonyms that are antonyms of each other: adhere (noun) **and** separate. (noun)

Coordinating conjunctions used to link verbs:

The dog <u>barked</u> **but** <u>stayed</u> to protect his bone.

verb verb

Coordinating conjunctions used to link adjectives:

He wore a <u>simple</u> **yet** <u>elegant</u> dress.

adjective adjective

Coordinating conjunctions used to link prepositional phrases:

Put the iguana <u>on the table</u> **or** <u>in the bathtub.</u>

prep. phrase prep. phrase

Coordinating conjunctions are also used to link complete ideas. Here are some examples. The conjunctions are in bold type.

<u>It's zero degrees outside today</u> **yet** <u>it's supposed to be twice as cold tomorrow.</u>

sentence sentence

<u>Don't sweat the petty things</u> **and** <u>don't pet the sweaty things.</u>

sentence sentence

<u>I'm not cheap,</u> **but** <u>I am on special this week.</u>

sentence sentence

A doctor gave a man six months to live. <u>The man couldn't pay his bill,</u> **so** <u>he gave him another six months.</u>

sentence

sentence

Drive It On Home

Circle the coordinating conjunction or conjunctions in each sentence.

1. In a perfect world, at least every once in a while, a kid who always closed the door softly would be told, "Go back and slam the door."
2. In a perfect world, highway patrolmen would never be around when you're running late, but they would always be at your side when a BMW blows past or a large truck won't get off your bumper.
3. In a perfect world, warranties would run thirteen months yet products would fail at twelve months.
4. In a perfect world, you would never fumble, but if you did, you would recover the ball yourself.
5. In a perfect world, the mail would always be early, the check would always be in the mail, and the check wouldn't bounce at the bank.

Come Again

As you learned in Chapter 2, *prepositions* connect words or groups of words. Sample prepositions include *in, on, under, for, at*. Prepositions are covered in detail in Chapter 5.

Answers:

1. and 2. but, or 3. yet 4. but 5. and

Show and Tell

Which conjunction should you choose to link your words and ideas? The rule is the same whether you're working with coordinating, subordinating, or correlative conjunctions: Choose the conjunction that best expresses your ideas. More on this later.

Subordinating Conjunctions

There are many different subordinating conjunctions, which is a handy thing, because each one expresses a different idea. Thus, each subordinating conjunction enables you to express your precise shade of meaning and avoid any misunderstandings. Here are some of the most common subordinating conjunctions:

after	although	as if	because
as long as	as soon as	as though	since
before	even though	in order that	till
so that	than	though	whenever
unless	until	when	
where	wherever	while	

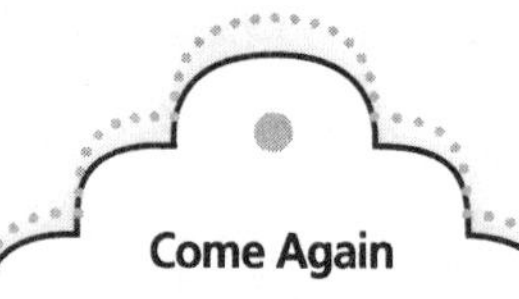

Come Again

An *independent clause* is a complete sentence. It has a subject, verb, and expresses a complete idea. A *dependent clause* is part of a sentence. It may have a subject, a verb, or even both, but it does not express a complete idea.

Using Subordinating Conjunctions

Subordinating conjunctions link a complete sentence (independent clause) to a part of a sentence (a dependent clause). Subordinating conjunctions link ideas by making one of the ideas subordinate to the other. To *subordinate* means "to place below in rank or importance."

The independent clause can come first or second in the sentence. That's your choice. Whether you place the independent clause first or second, try to place your most important ideas in the independent clause to give them emphasis. This

makes it easier for your readers or listeners to understand your main point. That's because you've given it top billing by making it the headliner. If the dependent clause comes first, set it off with a comma.

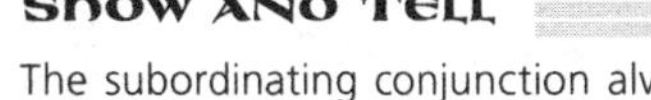

Show and Tell

The subordinating conjunction always comes immediately before the dependent idea.

The following sentences show the main idea in the independent clause. George W. Bush may have said them. Dan Quayle may have said them. I'll leave it to you, Gentle Reader, to figure out who said what. Remember me when you're playing this entertaining parlor game. The clauses are underlined and the subordinating conjunctions are in bold type.

"**If** we don't succeed, we run the risk of failure."

dependent clause — independent clause

"We have a firm commitment to NATO **because** we are part of NATO."

independent clause — dependent clause

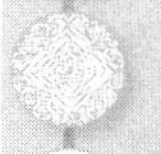

"We have a firm commitment to Europe **because** we are part of Europe."

independent clause — dependent clause

Drive It On Home

Circle the subordinating conjunction or conjunctions in each sentence of these common jokes.

1. I was just in London: There is a six-hour time difference. I'm still confused. When I go to dinner, I feel sexy. When I go to bed, I feel hungry.
2. A doctor says to a man, "You want to improve your love life? You need to get some exercise. Run ten miles a day." Two weeks later, the man called the doctor. The doctor says, "How is your love life since you have been running?" The man replies, "I don't know because I'm 140 miles away!"
3. If you had your life to live over again, spend it on a tropical island.
4. A man had his vasectomy done at Sears. Now as he makes love, the garage door goes up.
5. My son is twenty-one. He'll be twenty-two as long as I let him.
6. My son complains about headaches. I tell him all the time, when you get out of bed, it's feet first!
7. I've been in love with the same woman for forty-nine years. If my wife ever finds out, she'll kill me.
8. Hang in there because retirement is only thirty years away.
9. Why do you press harder on a remote control after you figure out that the battery is dead?
10. Why do they call it the Department of the Interior while they are in charge of everything outdoors?

Answers:

1. when, when	2. since, because	3. if	4. as
5. as long as	6. when	7. if	8. because
9. after	10. while		

Correlative Conjunctions

Correlative conjunctions link words or groups of words just as coordinating conjunctions do. However, unlike coordinating conjunctions, correlative conjunctions *always* work in pairs. Always. Here's the complete list of correlative conjunctions:

- both . . . and
- either . . . or
- neither . . . nor
- not only . . . but also
- whether . . . or

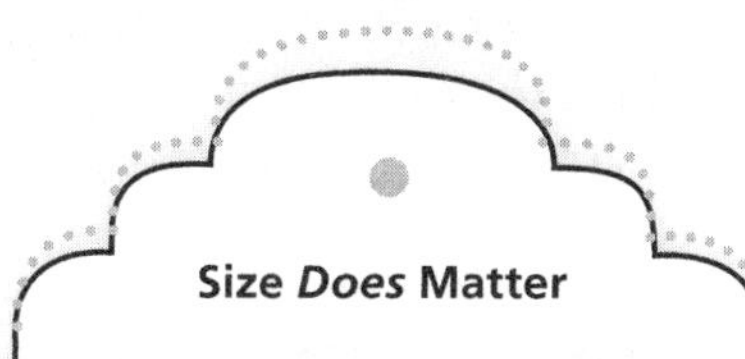

Size *Does* Matter

Here we go with the word recycling again: *after, before, since, till,* and *until* can function as subordinating conjunctions or prepositions. It all depends on the way the word is used in a sentence, as the following examples show:

Until you take out the trash, there's no nookie for you.
(Used as subordinating conjunction)

Until yesterday, I took out the trash.
(Used as preposition)

Using Correlative Conjunctions

Correlative conjunctions are lovely because they allow you to create logical and balanced sentences and show the relationship between ideas. This is because each correlative conjunction conveys a specific shade of meaning. For example, with the correlative conjunction *not only . . . but also*, the relationship is cause and effect. In the following examples, the correlative conjunctions are in bold type.

In a perfect world, if the guy from the government said to you, "I'm here to help," he would **not only** mean it, **but also** do it.

Both the lizard **and** the snake escaped.
Either you find the lizard **or** I'm sleeping at my mother's house tonight.

Drive It On Home

Circle the correlative conjunctions in each sentence.

1. Whether or not you agree, I'm inviting my parents for a visit.
2. The storm destroyed both the house and the boat.
3. Neither the elephant nor the hippo is welcome in the house.
4. Either the elephant or the hippo is going.
5. Lou finished not only the pie but also the ice cream.

Answers:

1. Whether . . . or
2. both . . . and
3. Neither . . . nor
4. Either . . . or
5. not only . . . . but also

Conjunctive Adverbs: An Adverb Pretending to Be a Conjunction

Conjunctive adverbs are used to connect other words. Technically speaking, they function as adverbs. Remember this when you're winning the million bucks on *Jeopardy.* A conjunctive adverb may be a single word like "also" or a phrase like "for example." Conjunctive adverbs act like conjunctions, even though they are not classified as conjunctions. Despite their tendency to be mislabeled, conjunctive adverbs are very useful when you want to make a transition between the different ideas that you are presenting. The following list shows some especially useful conjunctive adverbs.

accordingly	again	also
besides	consequently	finally
for example	furthermore	however
indeed	moreover	nevertheless
on the other hand	otherwise	then
therefore	thus	

Conjunctive adverbs, unlike the "real" conjunctions covered here, follow a pattern. It goes like this:

sentence semicolon conjunctive adverb comma sentence

In the following examples, the conjunctive adverbs are in bold type.

You overslept by an hour; **thus,** we left without you.
The car is unreliable; **for example**, it never starts in the rain.
Reruns of *I Love Lucy* are on tonight; **therefore**, I'm not budging from the couch.

Drive It On Home

Before we go on, let's pull it together. First, circle the conjunctions in each sentence. Then label each conjunction as coordinating, subordinating, or correlative.

1. My doctor grabbed me by the wallet and said, "Cough!"
2. Nurse: "Doctor, the man you just gave a clean bill of health to dropped dead right as he was leaving the office."
   Doctor: "Turn him around so people will think he was walking in."

3. You have a nice personality, but not for a human being.
4. He not only has a great personality but also an impressive wallet.
5. Is that your hat or are you wearing a cabana?
6. Either that dog goes or I do.
7. A dieter told me, "I haven't tasted food all week." I told him, "Don't worry because it still tastes the same."
8. Two women are living in New York. One says, "Do you see what's going on in Poland?" The other says, "I live in the back, so I don't see anything."
9. Those two are a fastidious couple. She's fast and he's hideous.
10. The room is so small, when I put the key in, I broke the window.

Answers:

1. and: coordinating
2. as: subordinating, so: coordinating
3. but: coordinating
4. not only . . . but also: correlative
5. or: coordinating
6. Either . . . or: correlative
7. because: subordinating
8. so: coordinating
9. and: coordinating
10. when: subordinating

Playing Nice with Others: Using Conjunctions to Link Ideas

As you've read in this chapter, you use conjunctions to show relationships between words, dependent clauses, and independent clauses. Using conjunctions makes your writing logical. Since the world rarely seems logical, you can compensate by having your speech and writing make sense. You'll be doing your share to make the world a smarter place.

Coordinate!

The following table shows the meaning of the seven coordinating conjunctions. Use the table to help you choose the exact conjunction to help you say just what you mean.

Having Fun with Coordinating Conjunctions

Coordinating Conjunctions	Meaning
and	linking
but	contrast
for	because
nor	negative
or	choice
so	result
yet	however

Subordinate!

The following table shows the meaning of some common subordinating conjunctions:

Making Hay with Subordinating Conjunctions

Subordinating Conjunctions	Meaning
unless, provided that, if, even if	condition
as, as if, because	reason
than, whether, rather than	choice
although, even though, but, though	contrast
where, wherever	location
in order that, so, so that, that	result/effect
after, as soon as, before, once, since, until, when, whenever, while	time

Use coordinating, subordinating, and correlative conjunctions to link related words and ideas. Strive to create logic and unity by your choice of conjunctions. In the following examples, the conjunctions are in bold type.

Short and choppy sentences:
I wish my brother would learn a trade.
I would know what kind of work he's out of.

Sentences joined with a coordinating conjunction for a better style:
I wish my brother would learn a trade, **so** I would know what kind of work he's out of.

Short and choppy sentences:
I take my husband everywhere.
He keeps finding his way back.

Sentences joined with a coordinating conjunction for a better style:
I take my husband everywhere, **but** he keeps finding his way back.

Short and choppy sentences:
Last night I ordered a whole meal in French.
The waiter was amazed.
It was a Chinese restaurant!

Sentences joined with a subordinating conjunction for a better style:
Last night I ordered a whole meal in French. The waiter was amazed **because** it was a Chinese restaurant!

Short and choppy sentences:
Pretty Boy Floyd was originally known for his bank robberies.

He gained even greater fame for his skill at avoiding police traps.

Sentences joined with a subordinating conjunction for a better style:
Although Pretty Boy Floyd was originally known for his bank robberies, he gained even greater fame for his skill at avoiding police traps.

Short and choppy sentences:
Male poison dart frogs carry fertilized eggs on their back.
The eggs hatch into tadpoles.

Sentences joined with a subordinating conjunction for a better style:
Male poison dart frogs carry fertilized eggs on their back **until** the eggs hatch into tadpoles.

Short and choppy sentences:
I know a man too cheap to pay for trash pickup.
He gift-wraps it.
He puts it into an unlocked car.

Sentences joined with a subordinating conjunction and a coordinating conjunction for a better style:
I know a man too cheap to pay for trash pickup **so** he gift-wraps it **and** puts it into an unlocked car.

A Note about the Semicolon

While we're here, let's take a moment to discuss the semicolon. This amazingly useful mark of punctuation has been given a bum rap, like carbs. The semicolon is easy to use and packs a nice wallop in a small package. Here's the basic guideline:

Use a semicolon to join two closely related independent clauses (complete sentences).

The semicolon looks like this: **;** . As you can see, it's a cross between a comma and a period. It has the comma's bewitching hesitancy and the period's alluring mastery. As such, it suggests a longer stop than a comma but a shorter stop than a period. It allows writers to link two complete sentences. A semicolon thus neatly solves the problem of a series of short, choppy sentences. Here are some examples:

Short and choppy sentences:
I know a man who is a diamond cutter.
He mows the lawn at Yankee Stadium.

Sentences joined with a semicolon for a better style:
I know a man who is a diamond cutter; he mows the lawn at Yankee Stadium.

Short and choppy sentences:
I played a great horse yesterday.
It took seven horses to beat him.

Sentences joined with a semicolon for a better style:
I played a great horse yesterday; it took seven horses to beat him.

Short and choppy sentences:
This is an elegant hotel.
Room service has an unlisted number.

Sentences joined with a semicolon for a better style:
This is an elegant hotel; room service has an unlisted number.

Togetherness Isn't All It's Cracked Up to Be

Combining related words and sentences gives your writing unity, cohesion, and logic. But more isn't always better. You'll often want a combination of short, medium, and long sentences to create rhythm and variety in your writing. In the following passage, we'll combine one sentence to make it long. Then we'll leave the last three short. The contrast between the long sentences in the beginning and the short ones at the end creates the rhythm of the sentence and make it far more effective.

Short and choppy sentences:

Three old ladies—Gertrude, Maude, and Tilly—were sitting on a park bench having a quiet conversation.

A flasher approached from across the park.

Sentences joined with a subordinating conjunction for a better style:

Three old ladies—Gertrude, Maude, and Tilly—were sitting on a park bench having a quiet conversation **when** a flasher approached from across the park.

Complete passage:

Three old ladies—Gertrude, Maude, and Tilly—were sitting on a park bench having a quiet conversation when a flasher approached from across the park. The flasher came upon the ladies, stood right in front of them, and opened his trenchcoat.

Gertrude immediately had a stroke.

Then Maude had a stroke.

But Tilly, being older and more feeble, couldn't reach that far.

Drive It On Home

Add a conjunction to each of the following sentences. The choice is yours; you may use coordinating, subordinating, or correlative conjunctions. You can even throw in a conjunctive adverb or two, if that makes you happy. Make your choices based on logic.

1. Office poster: ____________________ you do a good job and work hard, you may get a job with a better company someday.
2. Office poster: Sure, you may not like working here, ____________ we pay your rent.
3. Office poster: The beatings will continue ____________________ morale improves.
4. Office poster: There are two kinds of people in life: people who like their jobs ____________________ people who don't work here anymore.
5. ________________________ you finish watching TV, you can walk ____________________ the cat ________________________ the llama.
6. There was a huge traffic jam in town ____________________ we missed the beginning of the movie.
7. ____________________ you toss a penny 10,000 times, it will not be heads 5,000 times, ____________________ more like 4,950. The heads picture weighs more, ____________________ it ends up on the bottom.
8. He's ____________________ rich ____________________ single.
9. Ricardo would come to the party with us ____________________ , he has to work tonight.

10. This man is frank ______________________ earnest with women. In Fresno, he's Frank ______________________ in Chicago he's Ernest.

Sample Answers:

(The conjunctions are in boldface.)

1. Office poster: **If** you do a good job and work hard, you may get a job with a better company someday.
2. Office poster: Sure, you may not like working here, **but** we pay your rent.
3. Office poster: The beatings will continue **until** morale improves.
4. Office poster: There are two kinds of people in life: people who like their jobs **and** people who don't work here anymore.
5. **After** you finish watching TV, you can walk **both** the cat **and** the llama.
6. There was a huge traffic jam in town**; consequently,** we missed the beginning of the movie.
7. **If** you toss a penny 10,000 times, it will not be heads 5,000 times, **but** more like 4,950. The heads picture weighs more, **so** it ends up on the bottom.
8. He's **not only** rich **but also** single.
9. Ricardo would come to the party with us**; however**, he has to work tonight.
10. This man is frank **and** earnest with women. In Fresno, he's Frank **and** in Chicago he's Ernest.

Chapter 5

The NAUGHTY *Bits*

In this chapter, we'll explore prepositions and interjections. Prepositions aren't naughty (except when they're masquerading as adverbs, those cross-dressing tarts), but interjections are impish little creatures at best. As a result, they're prone to overuse and abuse, resulting in breathless prose.

Now, you'll get the lowdown on these two parts of speech. By the end of this chapter, you'll be using them with confidence and skill.

Big Name for a Little Pip-squeak: The Preposition

A *preposition* is a word that relates the noun or pronoun following it to another word. Don't be fooled by appearances: Even though prepositions are usually short words, they play a very important role in English. Why? Because they relate words. Here are some examples. The prepositions are in bold type in each sentence.

My horse was so late getting home, he tiptoed **into** the stable.
She's been married so many times she has rice marks **on** her face.
"Sweetbreads" are the thymus gland **of** an animal.

The following list shows some of the most common prepositions in English.

about	above	across	after
against	along	amid	among
around	as	at	before
behind	below	beneath	beside
besides	between	beyond	but
by	concerning	despite	down
during	except	for	from
in	inside	like	near
of	off	on	onto
opposite	out	outside	over
past	since	through	throughout
till	to	toward	under
underneath	until	up	upon
within	without		

SMARTY PANTS

To determine if a word is a preposition, ask yourself, "Is the word part of a phrase that ends in a noun or pronoun?" And stop moaning. This is a whole lot easier than asking yourself in the morning, "What day is this? Where the hell *am* I?"

Although most prepositions are individual words, a few prepositions are made up of several words. Not surprisingly, these are called *compound prepositions.* Here are the most common ones:

according to	ahead of	apart from	as of
aside from	because of	by means of	in addition to
in back of	in front of	in place of	in regard to
in spite of	instead of	in view of	next to
on account of	out of	owing to	prior to

Drive It On Home

Here's a list of jokes about resolutions you might want to consider next December 31. Circle the one preposition that you'll find in each of them.

New Year's Resolutions We Can Keep:

1. Stop exercising. It's just a waste of time.
2. Spend more time at work.
3. Take a vacation and visit the largest ball of twine.
4. Quit giving all that money and time to charity.
5. Eat cold pizza for breakfast.
6. Don't clean under the bed. (Who looks anyway?)
7. Only wear white T-shirts with those fashionable stains.
8. You know the stains, the ones under the arms.
9. Watch more TV during the day. You've been missing some good stuff.
10. Gain twenty pounds before February.

Answers:

1. of	2. at	3. of	4. to	5. for
6. under	7. with	8. under	9. during	10. before

Prepositional Phrases

Prepositions usually hang around in a group called a *prepositional phrase.* A prepositional phrase contains a preposition and a noun or pronoun. It may also contain adjectives and adverbs. As you can tell, a prepositional phrase can be as short as two words or as long as a really boring holiday dinner with the in-laws.

Following are some model prepositional phrases. The prepositions are in bold type and the prepositional phrases are underlined.

> Little Red Riding Hood walked <u>**into** the woods.</u>
>
> The wolf jumped out <u>**near** Granny's house.</u>
>
> The wolf ran <u>**from** Little Red Riding Hood.</u>

Prepositional phrases often describe relationships in time and space. In the following examples, the prepositions are in bold type and the prepositional phrases are underlined.

Time:

In <u>the spring</u>, we plant shrubs.

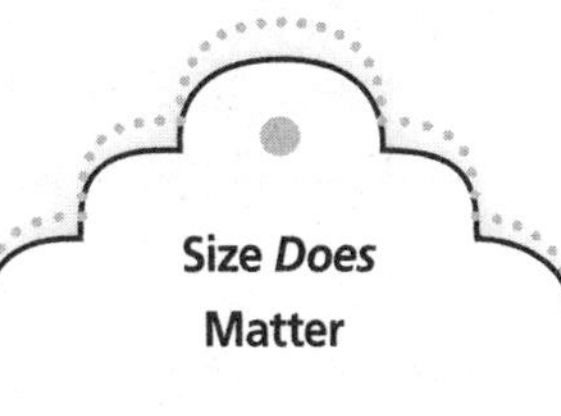

Size *Does* Matter

When you proofread, check that you have included all necessary prepositions. Since they're so small, prepositions are sometimes omitted. For instance:

Missing a preposition: The horse I bet on was so slow, the jockey kept a diary the trip.

Preposition added: The horse I bet on was so slow, the jockey kept a diary *of* the trip.

After the hurricane, we replace the shrubs.
Amid the drought, we replace them again.

SPACE:
Under the yum-yum tree, we found true love.
Near the airport, everyone wore earplugs.
John flies **to** Paris, the lucky stiff.

DRIVE IT ON HOME

Underline the prepositional phrase or phrases in each of these common riddles.

1. What do you call the best butter on the farm? *A goat.*
2. What do you get when you cross poison ivy with a four-leaf clover? *A rash of good luck.*
3. Where did the farmer take the pigs on Saturday afternoon? *He took them to a pignic.*
4. Where do fortune tellers dance? *At the crystal ball.*
5. What did one magnet say to the other? *I find you very attractive.*
6. What do you call a guy who's born in Columbus, grows up in Cleveland, and then dies in Cincinnati? *Dead.*
7. What do bees do with their honey? *They cell it.*
8. Why does the Easter Bunny have a shiny nose? *His powder puff is on the wrong end.*
9. Why was Cinderella thrown off the basketball team? *She ran away from the ball.*
10. What do you call a song sung in an automobile? *A cartoon.*

Answers:

1. on the farm
2. with a four-leaf clover; of good luck
3. on Saturday afternoon; to a pignic
4. At the crystal ball
5. to the other
6. in Columbus; in Cleveland; in Cincinnati
7. with their honey
8. on the wrong end
9. from the ball
10. in an automobile

Small but Powerful

Your choice of preposition affects the entire meaning of your sentence. Big time, too. Here are some examples that make my point. See how one itty-bitty preposition changes the entire meaning of the sentence:

Don't touch the cookies **near** the sink.
Don't touch the cookies **in** the sink.
Don't touch the cookies **by** the sink.
Don't touch the cookies **in front of** the sink.
Don't touch the cookies **in back of** the sink.
Don't touch the cookies **next to** the sink.
Don't touch the cookies **opposite** the sink.
Don't touch the cookies **over** the sink.
Don't touch the cookies **under** the sink.

That's because the preposition affects how the words relate to each other. There's a significant difference between "Don't touch the cookies **in** the sink" and "Don't touch the cookies **next to** the sink." Who would touch cookies *in* the sink? Eeeek!

Drive It On Home

Complete each sentence of this anecdote with an appropriate preposition.

1. It was Sunday, when the brain surgeon discovered a huge leak ______ his basement pipe.
2. He rushed ______ the stairs and called the plumber.
3. "Triple-A Plumbing? This is an emergency! Get ______ my house quickly!" the brain surgeon said.
4. "Okay, but I charge extra ______ Sunday emergency service," replied the plumber.
5. "Anything! Just stop this leak ______ the floor!" the brain surgeon replied.
6. The plumber arrived, took a tiny wrench ______ his bag, and lightly tapped the pipe. The leak stopped.
7. The plumber put a bill for $500 ______ the table.
8. "What?" screamed the surgeon. "That's unbelievable!" He collapsed ______ his chair.
9. "Why, I'm a brain surgeon and I don't make $500 ______ 5 minutes' work!" he screamed.
10. "I know," agreed the plumber as he walked ______ the door. "Neither did I when I was a brain surgeon."

Sample Answers:

1. It was Sunday, when the brain surgeon discovered a huge leak [in] his basement pipe.
2. He rushed [up] the stairs and called the plumber.
3. "Triple-A Plumbing? This is an emergency! Get [to] my house quickly!" the brain surgeon said.
4. "Okay, but I charge extra [for] Sunday emergency service," replied the plumber.
5. "Anything! Just stop this leak [beneath] the floor!" the brain surgeon replied.
6. The plumber arrived, took a tiny wrench [from] his bag, and lightly tapped the pipe. The leak stopped.
7. The plumber put a bill for $500 [on] the table.
8. "What?" screamed the surgeon. "That's unbelievable!" He collapsed [into] his chair.
9. "Why, I'm a brain surgeon and I don't make $500 [for] 5 minutes' work!" he screamed.
10. "I know," agreed the plumber as he walked [toward] the door. "Neither did I when I was a brain surgeon."

Drive It On Home

Rewrite each of the following vaudeville jokes, replacing each underlined preposition with a different one. Decide which version you prefer and why.

1. Getting on a plane, I told the ticket lady, "Send one <u>on</u> my bags <u>toward</u> New York, send one <u>toward</u> Los Angeles, and send one <u>toward</u> Miami."
   She said, "We can't do that!"

I told her, "You did it last week!"

2. The food on the plane was fit <u>to</u> a king. "Here, King!"
3. A drunk was <u>on front of</u> a judge. The judge says, "You've been brought here <u>by</u> drinking."

   The drunk says, "Okay, let's get started."
4. I was walking <u>by</u> the street, and I found a man's hand <u>on</u> my pocket.

   I asked, "What do you want?"

   He said, "A match."

   I said, "Why didn't you ask me?"

   He said, "I don't talk <u>at</u> strangers."
5. You look like a talent scout <u>by</u> a cemetery.

Sample Answers:

1. Getting on a plane, I told the ticket lady, "Send one [of] my bags [to] New York, send one [to] Los Angeles, and send one [to] Miami."

   She said, "We can't do that!"

   I told her, "You did it last week!"
2. The food on the plane was fit [for] a king. "Here, King!"
3. A drunk was [in front of] a judge. The judge says, "You've been brought here [for] drinking."

   The drunk says, "Okay, let's get started."
4. I was walking [down] the street, and I found a man's hand [in] my pocket. I asked, "What do you want?"

   He said, "A match."

   I said, "Why didn't you ask me?"

   He said, "I don't talk [to] strangers."
5. You look like a talent scout [for] a cemetery.

Location Is All

In Chapter 10, you'll discover the importance of placing adjectives and adverbs in the appropriate places in your sentences. If these modifiers (describers) are in the wrong position, your sentences won't convey your meaning. Worst of all, they might elicit a grin when you wanted grim. Following are some examples of misplaced prepositional phrases. The prepositional phrase is in bold type in each sentence.

Misplaced prepositional phrase:
The judge sentenced the killer to die in the electric chair **for the third time**.
(Error: This isn't *Die Another Day*. You can only die in the electric chair once, unless you're a cat with nine lives.)

Corrected sentence:
For the third time, the judge sentenced the killer to die in the electric chair.

Misplaced prepositional phrase:
Please take time to look over the letter that is enclosed **with your union representative**.
(Error: If your union representative is enclosed with a letter, we're talking a very thin union representative. Wonder how they folded him up?)

Corrected sentence:
Please take time **with your union representative** to look over the letter that is enclosed.

Misplaced prepositional phrase:
Tank had driven with his girlfriend Bunny from their home **in a Hummer** for the football game.

(Error: Yikes! Do Bunny and Tank live in a Hummer? Perhaps, but it's not likely.)

Corrected sentence:
Tank and his girlfriend Bunny had driven **in a Hummer** from their home for the football game.

Adverb or Preposition?

We're back to multipurpose words, my dears. Be brave: This will only hurt a little.

Remember that many English words can be different parts of speech, depending on the way they are used in a sentence. Yes, you guessed it: A preposition can also be an adverb, depending on how it is being used.

Remember: For a word to function as a preposition, it must be part of a prepositional phrase. Study the following examples:

Preposition:
The money flew out the window.
prepositional phrase: out the window

Adverb:
They went out.

Preposition:
The birds sang around us.
prepositional phrase: around us

Adverb:
See you around.

Preposition:
Remember when you necked behind the school?
prepositional phrase: behind the school

Adverb:
You left your worries behind.

Drive It On Home

Identify each underlined word as a preposition or an adverb. Circle your choice. Then write your reason.

1. Many idiots were diving off the cliff.

   preposition or adverb

   Reason: ______________________________

2. After I dropped the letter off, I remembered that I hadn't addressed it.

   preposition or adverb

   Reason: ______________________________

3. The fans wouldn't allow the rock star through.

   preposition or adverb

   Reason: ______________________________

4. He slipped through the screaming teenyboppers.

   preposition or adverb

   Reason: ______________________________

5. After the field trip, all the parents waited in the parking lot.

   preposition or adverb

   Reason: ______________________________

6. Even though the car was small, all six passengers fit in.

   preposition or adverb

   Reason: ______________________________

7. Before the divers went <u>below</u>, they checked all their equipment.

   preposition or adverb

   Reason: ______________________________

8. <u>Below</u> the water's surface, I saw a flock of mermaids.

   preposition or adverb

   Reason: ______________________________

9. As soon as he got home, he turned the TV <u>on.</u>

   preposition or adverb

   Reason: ______________________________

10. He enjoys watching TV, eating, and sleeping <u>on</u> his sofa.

    preposition or adverb

    Reason: ______________________________

Answers:

1.	preposition	"off the cliff" is the prepositional phrase.
2.	adverb	the word modifies (describes) the verb "dropped"
3.	adverb	the word modifies (describes) the verb "allow"
4.	preposition	"through the screaming teenyboppers" is the prepositional phrase.
5.	preposition	"in the parking lot" is the prepositional phrase.
6.	adverb	the word modifies (describes) the verb "fit."
7.	adverb	the word modifies (describes) the verb "went."
8.	preposition	"Below the water's surface" is the prepositional phrase.
9.	adverb	the word modifies (describes) the verb "turned."
10.	preposition	"on his sofa" is the prepositional phrase.

Interjections

An *interjection* expresses feeling or emotion. The key to remembering the function of an interjection lies in its name: To *interject* is to break in. These words are like party crashers: They weren't invited but they can add a little zip to an otherwise boring event. Interjections are not grammatically part of the sentence, so they are always set off from it by a comma or an exclamation mark, as the following examples show:

exclamation mark . . . . Wow! That's some cat you got there.
comma . . . . Well, if you insist.

Let Me Interject

Here are some of the most common interjections:

ah	darn	drat	for heaven's sake
gee	hey	no	oh
okay	ouch	uh	ugh
wow	yes		

Now, with great power come great responsibilities. Just because you have these powerful little bombs doesn't mean that you have to use them all the time in all your correspondence. Consider interjections like jalapeño peppers—a little goes a very long way. That's because interjections create a personal, informal, conversational tone. Here are some instances when interjections hit the spot:

- personal letters
- short stories
- journals and diaries
- e-mails
- novels

Chances are that you will use interjections rarely in writing, and that's perfectly okay. Matter of fact, that might be just dandy.

SMARTY PANTS

To determine if a word is an interjection, ask yourself, "Does the word express feeling or emotion? Does the word function independently of the sentence?"

Drive It On Home

Underline the interjections in these jokes.

1. An exasperated mother, whose son was always getting into mischief, finally asked him, "How do you expect to get into heaven?"
   The boy thought it over and said, "Well, I'll run in and out and keep slamming the door until Saint Peter says, 'For heaven's sake, Dylan, come in or stay out!'"
2. The doctor says, "You'll live to be sixty!"
   The patient replies, "I *am* sixty!"
   The doctor says, "See, what did I tell you?"
3. A man goes to a psychiatrist. The doctor says, "You're crazy."
   The man says, "I want a second opinion."
   The psychiatrist answers, "Okay, you're ugly, too."

4. A drunk goes up to a parking meter, puts in a quarter, and the dial goes to 60. The drunk says, "Huh! I lost 100 pounds!"
5. A bum asked me, "Can I have $300 for a cup of coffee?"
   I told him, "Coffee costs a dollar!"
   The bum said, "Yeah, but I want to drink it in Brazil!"
6. A honeymoon couple is in the Watergate Hotel in Washington. The bride is concerned. "What if the place is still bugged?" she asks.
   The groom says, "I'll look for a bug." He looks behind the drapes, behind the pictures, under the rug. "Aha!" he yells. Under the rug is a disk with four screws. He gets his Swiss army knife, unscrews the screws, and throws them out the window.
   The next morning, the hotel manager asks the newlyweds, "How was your room?"
   The groom says, "Why are you asking?"
   The hotel manager says, "Well, the people in the room under you complained the chandelier fell on them."
7. A guy complains of a headache. Another guy says, "Do what I do. I put my head on my wife's bosom, and the headache goes away."
   The next day, the man asks, "Did you do what I told you to?"
   "Yes, I sure did," the man answers. "By the way, you have a nice house!"
8. A person asked me, "How do you prepare for the stage?"
   I told her, "Well, it's like this. You go to diction school. They teach you to fill your mouth with marbles and talk right through the marbles. Each day you take one marble out. When you've lost all your marbles . . . "

Answers:

1. Well; For heaven's sake
2. See
3. Okay
4. Huh
5. Yeah
6. Aha; Well
7. Yes; By the way
8. Well

PART TWO

Be a Player

Chapter 6

PUNCTUATION: *A Little Dab Will Do Ya*

Here are two versions of a story that English teachers sometimes use to illustrate the value of punctuation. Both versions have the exact same words in the exact same order; only the punctuation has been changed. See for yourself what a big difference a little thing like punctuation can make:

Version #1:
Dear John:

I want a man who knows what love is all about. You are generous, kind, thoughtful. People who are not like you admit to being useless and inferior. You have ruined me for other men. I yearn for you. I have no feelings whatsoever when we're apart. I can forever be happy—will you let me be yours?

Harriet

VERSION #2:
Dear John:

I want a man who knows what love is. All about you are generous, kind, thoughtful people who are not like you. Admit to being useless and inferior. You have ruined me. For other men, I yearn. For you, I have no feelings whatsoever. When we're apart, I can forever be happy. Will you let me be?

Yours,
Harriet

As you can see, punctuation isn't a little thing at all. Rather, those little marks are vital to helping your readers understand your writing. They also help people who read aloud by showing them where to pause, where to stop, and where to change the inflection of their voice.

Luckily, the rules of punctuation are simple and easy to master. Once you understand them better, they will even make sense. Let's start with the three marks of punctuation that are used to signal the end of a sentence.

End Marks

English has three ways to show the end of a sentence: a period, a question mark, and an exclamation mark. All three marks are alike because they show the end of a complete thought. All three marks are different because they signal a different type of sentence.

Periods

A period is used at the end of a declarative or imperative sentence. Don't turn the page—these are just fancy words for simple ideas.

A *declarative sentence* states an idea. It's the most common sentence type.

My room is so small that the mice are hunchbacked.
You have the Midas touch. Everything you touch turns to a muffler.

An *imperative sentence* gives an order or a direction. It's a command.

Fasten your seat belt.
Take this road to save fifteen minutes.

Also use a period after an initial and most abbreviations. If the abbreviation comes at the end of the sentence, don't add another period. Here are some examples:

George W. Bush   Franklin D. Roosevelt   J. P. Morgan
Jr.   Sr.   Mr.   Ms.
B.A.   Ph.D.   A.M.   P.M.

An *acronym* is a word formed from initials and pronounced as a word. Don't use periods after each letter. For example:

scuba (self-contained underwater breathing apparatus)
NATO (North Atlantic Treaty Organization)

Question Marks

A question mark is used at the end of an *interrogative sentence*, a sentence that asks a question. If the quotation mark is part of dialogue, place it inside the closing quotation marks.

> A woman is taking a shower. There is a knock on the door. "Who is it?" she asks.
> "Blind man," he answers. Naked, the woman opens the door.
> He says, "Where do you want these blinds, lady?"

Exclamation Marks

An exclamation mark is used at the end of an *exclamatory sentence*, a sentence that conveys strong emotion.

> The omelet is ruined!
> Look at that clown!

Exclamation marks show strong emotion. Most professional writing is cool, like your relationship with your ex. Thus, exclamation marks are rarely used in most professional writing. Unless you're into bodice-ripper prose ("Look! There he was! The man of my dreams! Sven and his rippling muscles!"), steer clear of exclamation marks in most business documents.

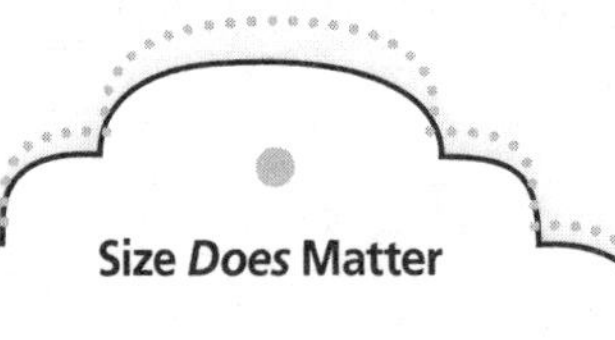

Size *Does* Matter

Don't be a piggy with end punctuation: You get only one of these at a time. Thus, you cannot follow an exclamation mark with a period or a question mark with an exclamation mark, for instance.

No-No: What do you call a pig that does karate?. A pork chop!.
Yes-Yes: What do you call a pig that does karate? A pork chop.

Drive It On Home

Add end marks as needed to the following riddles.

1. How do you make a hot dog stand
   Steal its chair
2. How do you prevent a summer cold
   Catch it in the winter
3. If a long dress is evening wear, what is a suit of armor
   Silverware
4. What bird can lift the most
   A crane
5. What bone will a dog never eat
   A trombone
6. What can you hold without ever touching it
   A conversation
7. What clothes does a house wear
   Address
8. What did one elevator say to the other
   I think I'm coming down with something
9. What country makes you shiver
   Chile
10. What do you call a calf after it's six months old
    Seven months old

Sample Answers:

You can use a period or an exclamation mark at the punch line of each riddle. I use a period to keep the jokes from sounding overwrought.

The Comma

As you've already learned in this chapter, three punctuation marks signal the end of a sentence. Other punctuation marks—especially the comma—help separate units of words within the sentence. The comma is the most-often used mark of punctuation within a sentence. Walk this way to use commas with confidence. . . .

Use Commas with Compound Sentences

A *compound sentence* is two or more independent clauses (complete sentences) joined by one of the seven coordinating conjunctions. You remember these folks: *but, and, nor, for, or, yet, so.* The comma goes directly before the coordinating conjunction. The pattern looks like this:

I take one day at a time, but sometimes several days attack me at once.

sentence — comma — coordinating conjunction — sentence

The coordinating conjunction is in bold type in the following sentences:

I'm on a new diet, coconuts and bananas.
I haven't lost weight, **but** I can climb a tree.
(sentence) (sentence)

Someone stole all my credit cards, **yet** I won't be reporting it.
(sentence) (sentence)

The thief spends less than I did.

A woman had two chickens. One got sick, **so** the woman made chicken soup out of the other one to help the sick one get well.

sentence sentence

Show and Tell

You can omit the comma in a very short compound sentence, like this one:

I smiled but he frowned.

Drive It On Home

Add commas as needed to the following compound sentences.

1. Thirty-five is when you really get your head together but your body starts falling apart.
2. The weather was terrible during our vacation yet we managed to see everything we wanted.
3. Bill Wilson and Robert H. Smith had a drinking problem so they joined forces in 1935 and started Alcoholics Anonymous.
4. Years ago, most athletes were recruited from the minors but now most athletes play college sports before moving on to the major leagues.
5. "I have made good judgments in the past and I have made good judgments in the future." (George W. Bush or Dan Quayle—take your pick)

Answers:

1. Thirty-five is when you really get your head together, but your body starts falling apart.
2. The weather was terrible during our vacation, yet we managed to see everything we wanted.
3. Bill Wilson and Robert H. Smith had a drinking problem, so they joined forces in 1935 and started Alcoholics Anonymous.
4. Years ago, most athletes were recruited from the minors, but now most athletes play college sports before moving on to the major leagues.
5. "I have made good judgments in the past, and I have made good judgments in the future."

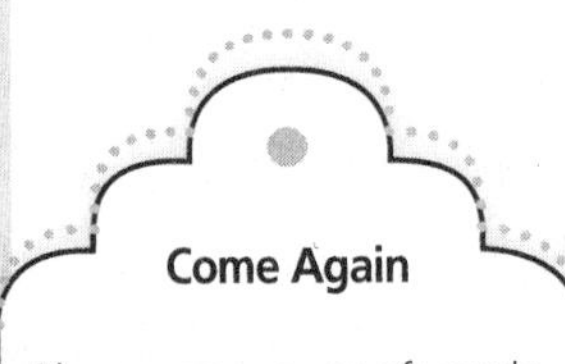

Come Again

Phrases are groups of words. *Clauses* are groups of words that have a subject and a verb. Phrases come in many different varieties; clauses may be *dependent* (cannot stand alone) or *independent* (a complete sentence).

Use Commas Between Items in a Row

Usually, you'll list three or more items. You can list individual words, like the items on a shopping list. You can also list phrases or clauses. The number of commas you use is always one less than the number of items. For instance, if you have three items, you use two commas.

Here's how it looks:

Series of words:

Our pets include a cat, dog, iguana, and hippo.

Series of phrases:

The hippo likes to wallow in the mud, enjoy a massage, and rest on the deck.

Series of clauses:

The children played basketball, the coaches kept score, the grandparents cheered, and the parents went out for drinks.

SMARTY PANTS

Technically, the comma before the coordinating conjunction in a list is optional, but get in the habit of using it all the time. Most people prefer it and you can't go wrong with a little consistency.

USE A COMMA WITH OPENING INFORMATION

Use a comma after any introductory word, phrase, or clause. This makes perfect sense because the comma shows that you are setting this information off from the rest of the sentence. In effect, the opening information interrupts the flow of the sentence. Here are some examples to use as models:

Introductory word:

Yes, I'd be delighted to stay for dinner.

No, I didn't know that you were serving snails and tofu soufflé.

Introductory phrase:

Over the rainbow, we saw a pot of gold.

In a perfect world, pro baseball players would complain about teachers being paid contracts worth millions of dollars.

Introductory clause:

"If we don't succeed, we run the risk of failure." (George W. Bush or Dan Quayle)

After you read the report, you will probably agree that we all deserve a vacation.

Drive It On Home

Add commas as needed to the following sentences.

1. Oh I didn't know you were here.
2. No I'm not upset that you're staying for six months.
3. To make your visit easier I've decided to visit Bora Bora for the duration.
4. Using my boundless ingenuity I'm traveling by rowboat.
5. After I return from my trip around the world I'll be sure to look you up.

Answers:

1. Oh, I didn't know you were here.
2. No, I'm not upset that you're staying for six months.
3. To make your visit easier, I've decided to visit Bora Bora for the duration.
4. Using my boundless ingenuity, I'm traveling by rowboat.
5. After I return from my trip around the world, I'll be sure to look you up.

Use a Comma to Set Off Nonessential Information

Use a comma to set off any information that's not necessary in the sentence. This information can take the form of interrupting words and expressions, words of direct address, or words and phrases that provide additional information. The nonessential information is in bold type in the following examples:

Interrupting words and expressions:

The rock star was accompanied, **of course**, by a hairdresser, makeup artist, and personal assistant.

She'll be on time, **I hope**.

Words of direct address:

"Direct address" means using a person's name to address him or her personally. The words of direct address can appear in the beginning, end, or middle of the sentence.

Harvey, did you hear about this new invention called deodorant? (word of direct address in the beginning of the sentence)

Did you hear about this new invention called deodorant, **Harvey**? (word of direct address at the end of the sentence)

Did you hear, **Harvey,** about this new invention called deodorant? (word of direct address in the middle of the sentence)

Words and phrases that provide additional information:

Babe Ruth, **whose salary in 1930–1931 was $80,000**, was the best-paid athlete of his time.

Ben-Hur, **starring Charlton Heston**, won more than ten Academy Awards.

Drive It On Home

Add commas as needed to the following sentences.

1. The movie *Frankenstein* produced by Thomas Edison was released in 1910.
2. The movie however was not a fan favorite.
3. Jean-Luc please be sure to take out the garbage before you go to outer space.
4. I'll get out the new warp drive Captain.
5. Hurricanes once given only men's names now get women's names as well.

Answers:

1. The movie *Frankenstein*, produced by Thomas Edison, was released in 1910.
2. The movie, however, was not a fan favorite.
3. Jean-Luc, please be sure to take out the garbage before you go to outer space.
4. I'll get out the new warp drive, Captain.
5. Hurricanes, once given only men's names, now get women's names as well.

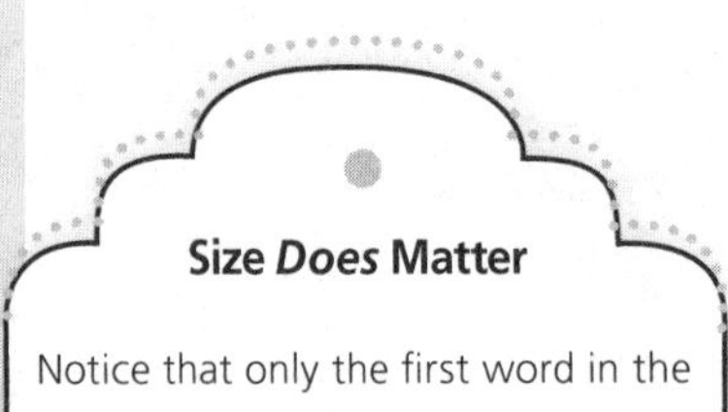

Size *Does* Matter

Notice that only the first word in the complimentary close is capitalized: We cap "Very" but not "truly" and not "yours." Follow this pattern.

Use Commas with Letters

Use a comma after the greeting of an informal letter.

Dear Mommy,
Dear Sweetcheeks,

Use a comma with the complimentary close of any letter.

Very truly yours,
Sincerely,

Use a Comma with Quotations

Use a comma to set off a direct quotation. Enjoy these examples:

The doctor calls Mrs. Smith and says, "Mrs. Smith, your check came back."

Mrs. Smith answers, "So did my arthritis."

A man pulls up to the curb and asks the policeman, "Can I park here?"

"No," says the cop.

The man asks, "What about all these other cars?"

"They didn't ask," the policeman answers.

Use Commas with Numbers

We'll finish with some minor housekeeping, using commas to keep numbers clear.

First, use a comma to separate the parts of an address.

321 Smith Road, Massapequa, New York 11735

Use a comma between the day of the month and the year.

August 2, 2004 April 5, 1974

Use commas to separate every three digits.

2,367 291,070 240,681,700

Colonoscopies: The Semicolon and Colon

The semicolon and colon inspire a level of dread previously reserved for mothers-in-law. Both mothers-in-law and semicolons/colons have gotten a bum rap. The former mean well and the latter do well. The rules are a snap.

Using Semicolons

Use a semicolon between independent clauses (complete sentences) when the coordinating conjunction has been left out. There are two ways to join independent clauses: with a coordinating conjunction (*but*, *and*, *nor*, *for*, *or*, *yet*, *so*) or with a semicolon. In the following examples, the coordinating conjunctions and semicolons are in bold type.

With a coordinating conjunction:
I'll buy anything marked down, **so** last year I bought an escalator.

Without a coordinating conjunction:
I'll buy anything marked down**;** last year I bought an escalator.

With a coordinating conjunction:
Laugh and the world laughs with you, **but** cry and you cry with your girlfriends.

Without a coordinating conjunction:
Laugh and the world laughs with you**;** cry and you cry with your girlfriends.

Use a semicolon to join independent clauses when one or both clauses contain a comma or a conjunctive adverb.

Clauses with commas:
"In politics, if you want anything said, ask a man**;** if you want anything done, ask a woman." (Margaret Thatcher)

Clauses with conjunctive adverbs:
We stopped for a drink with friends**;** as a result, we were late for dinner.

Using Colons

Easy, easy, easy! Only four rules for the colon, and they're a snap.

Size *Does* Matter

Be sure to join only those clauses that really fit together.

No-No: We stayed up all night watching *Star Trek;* we like fresh vegetables.
Yes-Yes: We stayed up all night watching *Star Trek;* who can resist Mr. Spock?

Rule #1: Use a colon before a list.

Liz plans to visit the following countries: France, Germany, Switzerland, and Ireland.

Rule #2: Use a colon before a long quotation, a quotation of more than five lines.

In *Letters from an American Farmer,* Hector St. John de Crèvecoeur wrote: "What, then, is the American, this new man? He is neither a European nor the descendent of a European; hence that strange mixture of blood, which you will find in no other country. I could point out to you a family whose grandfather was an Englishman, whose wife was Dutch, whose son married a French woman, and whose present four sons now have four wives of different nations. *He* is an American who, leaving behind him all his ancient prejudices and manners, receives new ones from the new mode of life he has embraced, the new government he obeys, and the new ranks he holds. He becomes an American by being received in the broad lap of our great Alma Mater. Here individuals of all nations are melted into a new race of men, whose labors and posterity will one day cause great changes in the world."

Rule #3: *Use a colon before part of a sentence that defines what was just stated.*

"The Tell-Tale Heart" opens this way: "True!—nervous—very, very dreadfully nervous I had been and am; but why will you say that I am mad? The disease had sharpened my senses—not destroyed—not dulled them. Above all was the sense of hearing acute. I heard all things in the heaven and in the earth. I heard many things in hell. How, then, am I mad? Hearken! And observe how healthily—how calmly I can tell you the whole story."

Rule #4: *Use a colon after the salutation of a business letter.*

Dear Dr. Samhle: Dear J. L. Rivera:

Drive It On Home

Add semicolons and colons as needed to these sentences.

1. A man's gotta do what a man's gotta do a woman must do what he can't.
2. "When women are depressed they eat or go shopping however when men are depressed they invade another country." (Elayne Boosler)
3. "Take this lesson to heart Nobody can make you feel inferior without your permission." (Eleanor Roosevelt)
4. "It isn't pollution that's harming the environment it's the impurities in our air and water that are doing it." (George W. Bush or Dan Quayle)
5. "One word probably sums up the responsibility of any governor 'to be prepared.'" (George W. Bush or Dan Quayle)

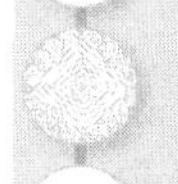

ANSWERS:

1. A man's gotta do what a man's gotta do; a woman must do what he can't.
2. "When women are depressed they eat or go shopping; however, when men are depressed they invade another country." (Elayne Boosler)
3. "Take this lesson to heart: Nobody can make you feel inferior without your permission." (Eleanor Roosevelt)
4. "It isn't pollution that's harming the environment; it's the impurities in our air and water that are doing it." (George W. Bush or Dan Quayle)
5. "One word probably sums up the responsibility of any governor: 'to be prepared.'" (George W. Bush or Dan Quayle)

Quotation Marks

You must remember this: Quotation marks show a speaker's exact words. Quotation marks always come in pairs. Now you have it.

Use quotation marks to set off a speaker's exact words.

The doctor says to the patient, "Take your clothes off and stick your tongue out the window."

"What will that do?" asks the patient.

The doctor says, "I'm mad at my neighbor."

Use quotation marks to set off the titles of short works such as poems, essays, songs, short stories, and magazine articles.

"The Road Not Taken"
"The Ransom of Red Chief"
"America the Beautiful"
"Better Sex in Six Days!"

Drive It On Home

Add quotation marks and additional commas as needed to make sense of the following joke:

Steven Spielberg is discussing his new project, an action docudrama about famous composers starring top movie stars. Sylvester Stallone, Steven Seagal, Bruce Willis, and Arnold Schwarzenegger are all present. Spielberg strongly desires the box-office power of these superstars, so he is prepared to allow them to select whatever composers they would portray, as long as they are very famous.

Well starts Stallone I've always admired Mozart. I would love to play him.

Chopin has always been my favorite, and my image would improve if people saw me playing the piano said Willis. I'll play him.

I've always been partial to Strauss and his waltzes said Seagal. I'd like to play him.

Looking at Schwarzenegger, Spielberg asks Who do you want to be Arnold?

Arnold says I'll be Bach.

Answer:

Steven Spielberg is discussing his new project, an action docudrama about famous composers starring top movie stars. Sylvester Stallone, Steven Seagal, Bruce Willis, and Arnold Schwarzenegger are all present. Spielberg strongly desires the box-office power of these superstars, so he is prepared to allow them to select whatever composers they would portray, as long as they are very famous.

"Well," starts Stallone, "I've always admired Mozart. I would love to play him."

"Chopin has always been my favorite, and my image would improve if people saw me playing the piano," said Willis. "I'll play him."

"I've always been partial to Strauss and his waltzes," says Seagal. "I'd like to play him."

Looking at Schwarzenegger, Spielberg asks, "Who do you want to be, Arnold?"

Arnold says, "I'll be Bach."

Other Cute Punctuation Marks

Let's round up the usual gang: the dash, hyphen, parentheses, brackets, and apostrophe.

The Dash and the Hyphen

A *hyphen* is one click, like this -
A *dash* is two clicks, like this —

Thus, the dash is twice as long as the hyphen. Size isn't all that separates them, though. The *dash* is used to show a sudden change of thought or a summary of what is stated in the sentence. Study the following examples:

The story involved two couples—but you don't want the whole story.
The star—if you can call her that—is good to her mother.

The *hyphen*, in contrast, is used to connect compound words.

father-in-law	un-American
one-third	eighty-eight

Parentheses and Brackets

Unlike Britney Spears and Jessica Simpson, parentheses and brackets are not interchangeable.

- These are *parentheses*: 
- These are *brackets*: 

Parentheses and brackets always come in pairs. But here's where the similarity ends: Parentheses and brackets are not at all the same.

Use parentheses to set off nonessential information and to enclose numbers or letters.

Alfred Hitchcock produced some horror films (including *The Birds*, *Psycho*, *Rear Window*) that are now considered classics.

The average American spends about 16 percent of each week (27 hours) watching TV.

Use brackets in the middle of a quote to correct an error or add clarification.

"The Civil War ended in 1864 [1865]."

Come Again

A *contraction* is created when two words have been combined by omitting letters from one or both of them. An apostrophe is inserted where the letter or letters have been omitted. Like wearing white shoes after Labor Day, using contractions is still not considered proper in some circles. This is especially true with formal writing, such as resumes, cover letters, and research papers.

Apostrophes

The apostrophe (') is used three ways:

- To show contractions
- To show plural forms
- To show possession (ownership)

Here's how it shakes down:

1. Use an apostrophe to show contractions.

The following chart shows some popular contractions and how they are formed.

Forming Contractions

Two Words	Contractions
I am	I'm
can not	can't
I will	I'll
he is	he's
you are	you're
I would	I'd

2. Use an apostrophe to show plural forms.

Use an apostrophe and *s* to write the plurals of numbers, symbols, letters, and words used to name themselves.

three 6's and five 9's

Just to play with your head, the *Chicago Manual of Style* favors "three 6s and five 9s." I say take your pick of style; just be consistent.

your *n*'s look like *h*'s

Again, the *Chicago Manual of Style* says it should be "your *n*s look like *h*s." But hey, they live in Chicago. It's so windy there that all the apostrophes probably blew away. Again, take your pick of style, but don't change midstream.

3. Use an apostrophe to show possession.

Add an apostrophe and an *s* to show the possessive case of most singular nouns. If the word ends in *s*, the second *s* can be dropped.

idea of the boy . . . . boy's idea
bone of the dog. . . . dog's bone
eye of the newt . . . . newt's eye
the car of James . . . James's car . . . or. . . . . . James' car

Add an apostrophe and an *s* to most plural nouns that don't end in *s* or *es.*

tantrums of the children. . . . children's tantrums
frustration of the people . . . . people's frustration

Add an apostrophe to show the possessive case of plural nouns ending in *s* or *es.*

the sand of the beaches . . . . beaches' sand
strokes of the swimmers. . . . . . . swimmers' strokes

Drive It On Home

Use an apostrophe to show the plural form of each noun.

1. the antics of Bozo ________________________________
2. the laundry of the men ____________________________
3. the room of Charles ______________________________
4. the gills of the tadpole ____________________________
5. the wages of Leroy ________________________________

Answers:

1. Bozo's antics
2. men's laundry
3. Charles's room or Charles' room
4. tadpole's gills
5. Leroy's wages

Drive It On Home

Kick up your heels and have some fun by adding punctuation as needed to the following joke.

A couple has been married thirty years The husband always insists on making love in the dark Finally driven crazy by curiosity the woman in the middle of a lovemaking session suddenly jumps off the bed and flips on the light She finds her husband holding a vibrator

A vibrator she cries angrily You impotent moron How could you do such a thing

The husband looks her straight in the eye and says I'll explain the vibrator You explain the kids

Answer:

A couple has been married thirty years. The husband always insists on making love in the dark. Finally, driven crazy by curiosity, the woman, in the middle of a lovemaking session, suddenly jumps off the bed and flips on the light. She finds her husband holding a vibrator.

"A vibrator!" she cries angrily. "You impotent moron! How could you do such a thing?"

The husband looks her straight in the eye and says, "I'll explain the vibrator. You explain the kids."

Chapter 7

Capital Punishment It Ain't: CAPITALIZATION *and* ABBREVIATION

English has both lowercase letters and uppercase letters. We also call the uppercase ones "capital letters." How come? The term *uppercase* comes from the days of metal type. The lesser-used capital letters were kept in the harder-to-reach upper cases while the more frequently used letters were kept nearer at hand in the lower cases.

We're long past cases of metal type, but we still have a fixed system of capital and lowercase letters. It's a capital idea, so let's review the rules. (And while we're here, we'll go over abbreviations as well.)

Capital Gain

Capital letters may seem to be just one more thing that was invented to make your life annoying, like hangnails or jock itch, but capital letters actually serve a purpose. Capital letters signal specific and distinct relationships. They help us make sense out of words. As a result, we follow them carefully. Here's how they work.

Capitalize the First Word in a Sentence

Remember: A sentence can take different forms. It can be declarative (statement), imperative (command), interrogative (question), exclamatory (exclamation). Whether the sentence ends with a period, a question mark, or an exclamation mark, it still starts with a capital letter. The sentence can be a quotation, too. Here are some examples:

Sentences:

My brother was a lifeguard in a car wash.
Please close the door on your way out.
What did you say your name was?
Did you see the size of that car?

Quotations:

While impatiently waiting for a table in a restaurant, Mrs. Smith said to Mrs. Jones, "If they weren't so crowded here all the time, they'd do a lot more business."

Kathleen came home from a Women's Liberation meeting and told her husband that the meeting had been about free love.
"Surely," he said, "you don't believe in free love?"
"Have I ever sent you a bill?" she replied.

After a Colon (when the colon is followed by a complete sentence):

We all had the same reaction: How could we tell her that she had missed the season finale of *Sex and the City*?

Size *Does* Matter

Only capitalize the first word of a quotation if the quotation is a complete sentence. Ditto on sentences after colons. We're working with sentences here, not fragments.

Drive It On Home

Add capital letters as needed to the following sentences.

1. my wife and I went to a hotel where we got a waterbed. my wife called it the Dead Sea.
2. the famous last words of General John Sedgwick, shot at the Battle of Spotsylvania Courthouse, Virginia, while looking over the balcony at the enemy lines: "they couldn't hit an elephant at this dist—."
3. a woman says to a man, "i haven't seen you around here."
   "yes, I just got out of jail for killing my wife."
   "so you're single. . . ."
4. what did the rug say to the floor? don't move: i've got you covered.
5. you know you are addicted to your computer if you e-mail the person who works at the desk next to you.
6. the roommates agreed on some ground rules: no singing before 9:00 A.M., no drinking directly from the milk carton, and no leaving the toilet seat up.
7. my wife and I have the secret to making a marriage last. two times a week, we go to a nice restaurant, a little wine, good food. . . . she goes Tuesdays, I go Fridays.
8. i just finished my income tax forms. who says you can't get wounded by a blank?
9. they spent all day buying shower gifts: inflatable dolls, edible underpants, and handcuffs.
10. two guys are in a health club, and one is putting on pantyhose. "since when do you wear pantyhose?" asks the first guy.
    "since my wife found it in the glove compartment," answers the second one.

Answers:

1. My wife and I went to a hotel where we got a waterbed. My wife called it the Dead Sea.
2. The famous last words of General John Sedgwick, shot at the Battle of Spotsylvania Courthouse, Virginia, while looking over the balcony at the enemy lines: "They couldn't hit an elephant at this dist—."
3. A woman says to a man, "I haven't seen you around here."
   "Yes, I just got out of jail for killing my wife."
   "So you're single. . . ."
4. What did the rug say to the floor? Don't move: I've got you covered.
5. You know you are addicted to your computer if you e-mail the person who works at the desk next to you.
6. The roommates agreed on some ground rules: No singing before 9:00 A.M., no drinking directly from the milk carton, and no leaving the toilet seat up.
7. My wife and I have the secret to making a marriage last. Two times a week, we go to a nice restaurant, a little wine, good food. . . . She goes Tuesdays, I go Fridays.
8. I just finished my income tax forms. Who says you can't get wounded by a blank?
9. They spent all day buying shower gifts: inflatable dolls, edible underpants, and handcuffs.
10. Two guys are in a health club, and one is putting on pantyhose. "Since when do you wear pantyhose?" asks the first guy.
    "Since my wife found it in the glove compartment," answers the second one.

Capitalize Proper Nouns

Remember: Proper nouns and proper adjectives aren't words that behave well in public. Rather, they're words that name a specific person, place, or thing. The rule is simple: Capitalize all proper nouns and proper adjectives. We'll treat proper adjectives later in this lesson.

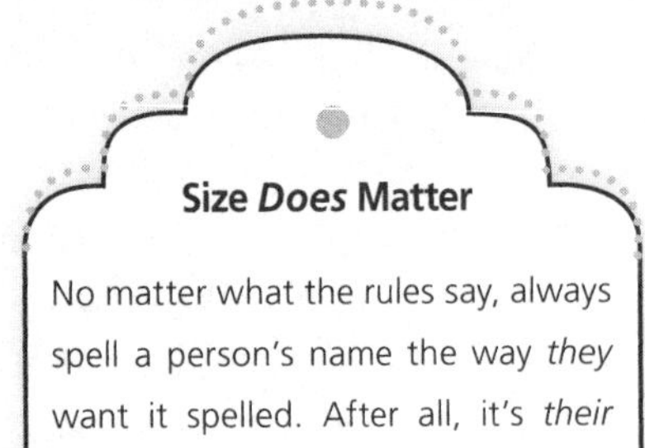

Size *Does* Matter

No matter what the rules say, always spell a person's name the way *they* want it spelled. After all, it's *their* name!

Names:

Judge Crater	Henry L. Stimson
Garfield the cat	Odie the dog
Pee-wee Herman	Herman Munster
Bozo	Master Baty

A few eccentric people prefer to write their names with no capital letters at all. Examples include the poet e.e. cummings and singer k.d. lang. Each to his own taste, as the cannibal said to the missionary. These usages should be respected, no matter how strange they are. (Remember the singer formerly known as "Prince"?)

Show and Tell

In general, if a last name begins with *Mc, O',* or *St.,* capitalize the next letter as well: *McMannus, O'Neill, St. Claire.* If the name begins with *la, le, Mac, van, von, de, or D',* the capitalization varies: *le Blanc* and *Le Blanc* are both correct versions, for example.

Places:

Plitt Avenue
Crapo, Maryland
Purgatory, Maine
the Canary Islands
Boogertown, North Carolina
Hellhole, Idaho
Death Valley
the Amazon River

Show and Tell

Capitalize a compass point when it identifies a specific area of the country, as in this example: "Cowboys live in the West." Don't capitalize a compass point when it refers to direction: "The airplane comes from the east."

Historical Events:

the Middle Ages
the Magna Carta
the Civil War

Calendar Events:

Tuesday
April
Groundhog Day
Purim
Thanksgiving

Drive It On Home

Add capital letters as needed to the following sentences.

1. what did tennessee?
   the same thing arkansas.
   what did delaware?
   her new jersey.
2. pat opened a furniture store in london and was highly successful. to celebrate, he went on holiday to paris. meeting fred at his favorite pub

after returning, he said, "fred, old chap, i just returned from a glorious holiday in paris."

"you don't say. why'd you go to paris, paddy, when you don't speak french?"

"i know, but i got along okay. i met a beautiful mam'selle in a park. i took out my paper and pen and drew a picture of a plate, knife, and fork. she accepted, and we went to a dimly lit café and enjoyed a sumptuous meal. after dinner, i drew a picture of a musical note and trumpet, and we went to a cabaret and drank, danced, and made merry. at midnight, she took the pen and paper and drew a picture of a bed. . . ."

"dash it all, paddy. how'd she know you owned a furniture store?"

3. george bernard shaw was at one time more celebrated as a music critic than as a playwright. one night, he was eating in a restaurant where the orchestra was inferior. the bandleader asked shaw what he would like the musicians to play next. shaw replied, "dominoes."
4. calvin coolidge, the man from vermont who became the thirtieth president of the united states, had a reputation for saying as little as possible. one story involves a friend who had missed a sermon on sin that coolidge had attended. the friend asked coolidge what the preacher had said about sin. coolidge replied, "he said he was against it."
5. when she was told that coolidge had died, dorothy parker, the famous new york wit, asked, "how can you tell?"
6. what do you get if you cross an insect with the easter rabbit?
   bugs bunny.

7. from wednesday to saturday, we plan on taking a trip from las vegas, nevada, to lake powell.
8. during the renaissance, queen elizabeth i ruled england.
9. on labor day, the town of frostbite falls, minnesota, sets off firecrackers amid flying squirrels.
10. in tombstone, arizona, on the grave of a wells fargo agent:
    here lies
    lester moore
    four slugs
    from a .44
    no less
    no more.

Answers:

1. What did Tennessee?
   The same thing Arkansas.
   What did Delaware?
   Her New Jersey.
2. Pat opened a furniture store in London and was highly successful. To celebrate, he went on holiday to Paris. Meeting Fred at his favorite pub after returning, he said, "Fred, old chap, I just returned from a glorious holiday in Paris."

   "You don't say. Why'd you go to Paris, Paddy, when you don't speak French?"

   "I know, but I got along okay. I met a beautiful mam'selle in a park. I took out my paper and pen and drew a picture of a plate, knife,

> and fork. She accepted, and we went to a dimly lit café and enjoyed a sumptuous meal. After dinner, I drew a picture of a musical note and trumpet, and we went to a cabaret and drank, danced, and made merry. At midnight, she took the pen and paper and drew a picture of a bed. . . ."

"Dash it all, Paddy. How'd she know you owned a furniture store?"

3. George Bernard Shaw was at one time more celebrated as a music critic than as a playwright. One night, he was eating in a restaurant where the orchestra was inferior. The bandleader asked Shaw what he would like the musicians to play next. Shaw replied, "Dominoes."
4. Calvin Coolidge, the man from Vermont who became the thirtieth president of the United States, had a reputation for saying as little as possible. One story involves a friend who had missed a sermon on sin that Coolidge had attended. The friend asked Coolidge what the preacher had said about sin. Coolidge replied, "He said he was against it."
5. When she was told that Coolidge had died, Dorothy Parker, the famous New York wit, asked, "How can you tell?"
6. What do you get if you cross an insect with the Easter rabbit?
   Bugs Bunny.
7. From Wednesday to Saturday, we plan on taking a trip from Las Vegas, Nevada, to Lake Powell.
8. During the Renaissance, Queen Elizabeth I ruled England.
9. On Labor Day, the town of Frostbite Falls, Minnesota, sets off firecrackers amid flying squirrels.
10. In Tombstone, Arizona, on the grave of a Wells Fargo agent:

Here lies
Lester Moore
four slugs
from a .44
no less
no more.

Size *Does* Matter

Capital and *Capitol* are often confused and misused. *Capital* means "the official seat of government for a country, state, etc.," "the net worth of a business," "excellent or first-rate," "involving the loss of life," "a type of letter." *Capitol* means "the building in Washington, D.C., in which the U.S. Congress holds its sessions." If *capitol* is lowercase, it refers to the building or buildings in which a state legislature meets.

Capitalize Organizations, Languages, and Religious References

These all get capital letters because they're all proper nouns. Here are some examples:

Organizations:
Lions Club
Parent-Teacher Association
Hofstra University
Democratic Party

Languages:
English
Swahili
Italian
Hebrew

What about foods that have a proper noun in their title? Most of the time, these are proper nouns for nationalities or languages. For instance, is it *danish pastry* or *Danish pastry*? *Russian dressing* or *russian dressing*? This issue is more hotly debated than the question of double-dipping in the French (french?) onion sour cream dip. No one's duked it out yet. Here's your rule of thumb: Be consistent. Always capitalize them or never capitalize them, but don't keep switching back and forth.

School subjects do not get capitalized unless they're languages or specific courses. The following chart lays it all out. (Notice that languages are *always* capitalized.)

Capitalizing Subjects and Classes

Subjects	Classes
history	World History 9
geography	Geography 101
science	Biology and Physiology
math	Algebra
English	English
German	German
Latin	Latin

Size *Does* Matter

Don't capitalize the words "god" or "goddess" when they refer to ancient mythology, as these examples show: the goddess Diana, the god Zeus.

Religious References:

God

His love

the Torah

Brahma

Buddha

Capitalize Special Places and Items

Since we're still on proper nouns, the same rules apply: They get capped.

Special Places:	Special Items:
Statue of Liberty	Nobel Peace Prize
Chrysler Building	Model T
Venus	Kleenex™
Golden Gate Bridge	

Trademarks present a special issue. Brand names that have become so successful that they have passed into common usage (such as Kleenex™ and Band-Aids™) must be capitalized. Further, they should not be bandied about since they are trademarked. Instead of Kleenex™, use "tissues" or "facial tissues"; instead of Band-Aids™, use "bandages." This isn't something to take lightly, buckaroos, since manufacturers can take legal action against people who use their trademarks without permission.

Capitalize Titles

Since they show respect, a person's title is also capitalized, as the following examples show:

Ms. Steinem
Miss Sweet Potato
Rabbi Schwartz
Dr. Quack

Capitalize Proper Adjectives

Capitalize most proper adjectives. Here are some examples:

Paris manners
Japanese people
Victorian books

Don't capitalize the prefix attached to a proper adjective unless the prefix refers to a nationality. For example: all-American, Anglo-Saxon.

Drive It On Home

Add capital letters as needed to the following sentences.

1. marci took french, spanish, calculus ii, and math. she also joined the girl scouts, the campfire girls, and the future teachers of america. busy girl, that marci.
2. minister jones, rabbi klein, and father kelly were sitting in a rowboat looking at the big dipper in the milky way.
3. the sears tower is a nifty place.
4. herman applied to williams college, adelphi university, and columbia university.
5. leroy once flew to paris on the *concorde.* he took pictures of the french dressing on his salad with his kodak instamatic™.
6. in ancient mythology, the goddess athena was the giver of wisdom.
7. the white house gives free tours.

8. many french-speaking canadians live in montreal.
9. i like french toast dripping with vermont maple syrup.
10. professor carman, sergeant wilson, and lord ashton-smyth visited the ellis island museum.

Answers:

1. Marci took French, Spanish, Calculus II, and math. She also joined the Girl Scouts, the Campfire Girls, and the Future Teachers of America. Busy girl, that Marci.
2. Minister Jones, Rabbi Klein, and Father Kelly were sitting in a rowboat looking at the Big Dipper in the Milky Way.
3. The Sears Tower is a nifty place.
4. Herman applied to Williams College, Adelphi University, and Columbia University.

5. Leroy once flew to Paris on the *Concorde.* He took pictures of the French dressing on his salad with his Kodak Instamatic™.

6. In ancient mythology, the goddess Athena was the giver of wisdom.
7. The White House gives free tours.

8. Many French-speaking Canadians live in Montreal.
9. I like French toast dripping with Vermont maple syrup.
10. Professor Carman, Sergeant Wilson, and Lord Ashton-Smyth visited the Ellis Island Museum.

Capitalize Parts of Correspondence

This is done as a convention, to set off the specific part of the document. The rules for capitalizing parts of e-mail correspondence are still evolving.

Capitalize the first word and all nouns in a salutation.
Dear Ms. Wombat:
My Dear Friend,

Capitalize the first word in a complimentary close.
With best regards,
Very sincerely yours,

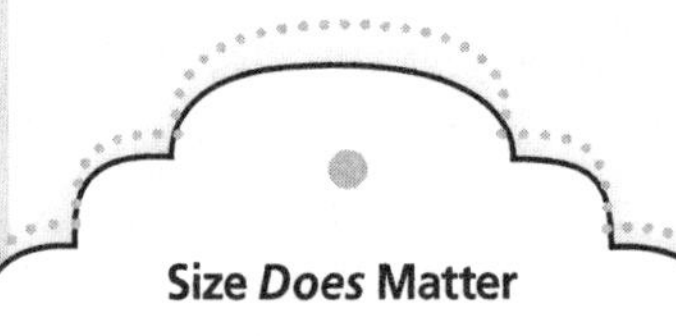

Size *Does* Matter

Using unnecessary capital letters makes writing look very silly. Here's an example:

Your Eternal Vision is linked by a Crystal Entity to the Eighth Circle of the Astral Plane, from where the Intuitive Spirit is transmitted to your True Soul.

Drive It On Home

Add capital letters as needed to the following letter.

march 15, 2004

ms. m. susan wilson
northern lights magazine
editorial and production offices
5120 w. smith st., suite 3
seattle, wa 98108

dear ms. wilson:

"studies reveal that people's number one fear is public speaking. death is number two. does that seem right? that means to the

average person, if you have to go to a funeral, you're better off in the casket than doing the eulogy." (jerry seinfeld)

i'd like to write an article for *northern lights magazine* on public speaking for business executives. the article would give concise, practical advice about writing and delivering a speech.

the enclosed resume offers a brief overview of my publications. i have published more than 100 books—50+ are currently for sale in bookstores and on amazon.com—as well as numerous articles. in addition, i've lectured nationally and have appeared on a wide variety of television and radio shows, including *the cbs morning show, the maury povich show,* and *live with regis and kelly.*

thank you for your time and i hope we can work together soon.

sincerely,
laurie rozakis, ph.d.

SMARTY PANTS

In all things grammatical, tastes change. A hundred years ago, for instance, it was common to use far more capital letters than we do today. Here's an example from the opening of Charles Dickens's *A Tale of Two Cities:* "It was the best of times, it was the worst of times, it was the age of wisdom, it was the age of foolishness, it was the epoch of belief, it was the epoch of incredulity, it was the season of Light, it was the season of Darkness . . ." Today we would not capitalize "light" and "darkness."

Answer:

March 15, 2004

Ms. M. Susan Wilson
Northern Lights Magazine
Editorial and Production Offices
5120 W. Smith St., Suite 3
Seattle, WA 98108

Dear Ms. Wilson:

"Studies reveal that people's number one fear is public speaking. Death is number two. Does that seem right? That means to the average person, if you have to go to a funeral, you're better off in the casket than doing the eulogy." (Jerry Seinfeld)

I'd like to write an article for *Northern Lights Magazine* on public speaking for business executives. The article would give concise, practical advice about writing and delivering a speech.

The enclosed resume offers a brief overview of my publications. I have published more than 100 books—50+ are currently for sale in bookstores and on Amazon.com—as well as numerous articles. In addition, I've lectured nationally and have appeared on a wide variety of television and radio shows, including *The CBS Morning Show, The Maury Povich Show,* and *Live with Regis and Kelly.*

Thank you for your time and I hope we can work together soon.

Sincerely,
Laurie Rozakis, Ph.D.

SMARTY PANTS

You can capitalize an entire word or phrase to emphasize it, as in ABSOLUTELY NO TALKING. However, this is often considered rude—especially in e-mail—and should usually be avoided.

Short 'n' Sweet: Abbreviations

Alphabets—in which each symbol stands for a single sound or a small group of sounds—are a far more economical method of representing a language than syllabaries or pictographic scripts, in which the symbols stand for syllables or words. Abbreviations are even more economical because they shorten an existing word. Clever, eh?

Here are the rules for using abbreviations.

1. Don't make up your own abbreviations. Use only conventional, standard, tried-and-true abbreviations. This is not the creative part of creative writing.
2. Don't use e-mail abbreviations in conventional documents. None of this *4* for "four," its bastard offspring *b/4* for "before," and my personal Idaho, *u* for "you."
3. Do abbreviate titles of people, such as *Mr.* (for "Mister") and *Dr.* (for "Doctor").
4. Do abbreviate time, such as *a.m.* (for "ante meridiem," before noon) and *p.m.* (for "post meridiem," after noon). These abbreviations are acceptable with and without periods.

5. Do abbreviate historical dates, such as *b.c.e.* (for "before the Common Era") and *a.d.* (for "anno Domini," in the year of the Lord). b.c.e. comes after the date; a.d. comes before the date. They are written like this: 53 b.c.e. and a.d. 14.
6. Do abbreviate academic degrees, such as *B.A.* or *A.B.* (for "Bachelor of Arts" or "Baccalaureus Artium") and *Ph.D.* (for "Doctor of Philosophy").
7. Do abbreviate geographical terms after a proper noun, such as *Ave.* (for "Avenue"), *St.* (for "Street"), and *Mt.* (for "Mountain"). These abbreviations can come before or after the noun, as in *Main St.* or *Mt. Hood.*
8. Do abbreviate states, such as *CA* (for "California") and *AK* (for "Arkansas"). These abbreviations do *not* take a period.
9. Do abbreviate measurements, such as *yd.* (for "yard"), *F* (for "Fahrenheit"), and *m* (for "meter"). Some of these abbreviations take a period but others do not. If in doubt, consult a dictionary.
10. Do abbreviate Latin words such as *e.g.* (for "for example") and *i.e.* (for "that is").

Drive It On Home

Write the abbreviation for each word.

1. ounce
2. Doctor of Medicine
3. New Mexico
4. road
5. Pennsylvania
6. Registered Nurse

7. Arizona
8. inch
9. pound
10. Fort

Answers:

1. oz.
2. M.D.
3. NM
4. Rd.
5. PA
6. R.N.
7. AZ
8. in.
9. lb.
10. Ft.

Chapter 8
Spelling: SPELL IT RITE

Here's an old joke that demonstrates the importance of writing words correctly:

A long time ago, a young monk arrives at the monastery. He is assigned to help the other monks copy the old church laws. Of course, this was all done by hand. The new monk notices that all the other monks are copying from copies, not the original manuscripts. The new monk questions the head abbot about this, and he points out that if someone made a small error in the first copy, it would never be picked up. In fact, that error would be continued in all subsequent copies. The head monk says, "We have been copying from the copies for centuries, but you make a good point, my son."

The head monk goes down into the old caves underneath the monastery where the original manuscripts are held in a locked vault that hasn't been opened for centuries. Hours go by and no one sees the abbot.

The young monk gets worried and goes into the vault to look for the abbot. He sees the old man banging his head against the wall and wailing, "We forgot the *r*; we forgot the *r*." He is sobbing uncontrollably. The young monk asks the abbot, "What is wrong, father?"

In a choking voice, the old abbot replies, "The word is celeb*r*ate; the word is celeb*r*ate."

Still smarting from the way you misspelled *arguing* in the fifth grade? Glad you got married so you don't have to spell *bachelor* again? Know that you graduated from college but can't remember if you're an *alumnus* or an *alumna*? Done some rude things to *potato*, like my spelling hero Dan Quayle? If so, roll up your sleeves. We've got some work to do.

Spelling Rules

Unlike your ex-husband or ex-wife, spelling rules work. Below are several time-honored spelling rules that can help you deal with a lot of (spelling) demons.

Sing Along with Me

This one's as traditional as "Spin the Bottle" (and a whole lot more fun, unless you got to kiss the seventh-grade hottie):

i before *e* except after *c*,
or as sounded as *a* as in *neighbor* and *weigh*.

Here are some words that fit the rule:

The "*I* Before *E*" Rule

i before *e*	except after *c*	or as sounded as *a*
achieve	ceiling	beige
believe	conceit	eight
bier	conceive	feint
chief	deceit	freight
fiend	deceive	heir
fierce	inconceivable	neighbor
grief	perceive	reign
piece	receipt	sleigh
relieve	receive	surveillance
shriek	subceiling	veil
yield	transceiver	weigh

Alas! Not all words with this pattern fit this rule. Following are some common exceptions:

counterfeit	protein
either, neither	seize
foreign	Fahrenheit
height	glacier
leisure	weird

Show and Tell

In most cases, when the *c* sounds like *sh,* the order of the letters is *ie,* not *ei.* Words that fit this rule include the following: *ancient, efficient, conscientious.*

The "–ceed/–cede" Rule

Only one English verb ends in *–sede*: *supersede*. Only three verbs in English end in *–ceed*: *succeed*, *proceed*, *exceed*. All the other verbs with that sound end in *–cede*. For example:

accede
concede
intercede
recede
secede

The "–ful" Rule

The sound *full* at the end of a word is spelled with only one *l*. The one exception to the "full" rule is the word *full* itself! Here are some examples of words that follow this rule:

The "–ful" Rule in Action

Root Word	Suffix	New Word
care	ful	careful
grace	ful	graceful
health	ful	healthful
hope	ful	hopeful

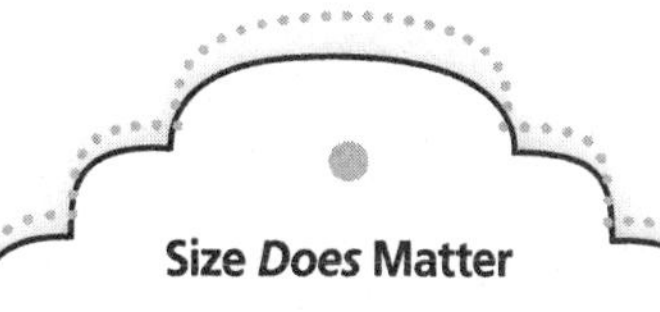

Size *Does* Matter

Also be on the lookout for words with silent letters, like *February, laboratory,* and *chocolate*. Remember this famous story: Jean Harlow, the Hollywood sex goddess, insisted on addressing the patrician Margot, Lady Asquith, by her first name. This might have been a sufficient social offense, but Harlow made it worse by pronouncing the *t* at the end of "Margot." Tiring of this ignorant impertinence, Lady Asquith set Harlow straight with this retort: "My dear, the *t* is silent—as in *Harlow*."

When the suffix is *–ful* plus *–ly*, there are two *l*'s. Following are some examples:

Still Full of It

Root Word	Suffix	New Word
restful	ly	restfully
baleful	ly	balefully
thankful	ly	thankfully
mirthful	ly	mirthfully
artful	ly	artfully
zestful	ly	zestfully

***–ery* OR *–ary*?**

Stumped when to use *–ery* or *–ary* at the end of a word? Try these guidelines. First of all, only five commonplace words end with *–ery* as opposed to *–ary*. And here they are:

cemetery
millinery
monastery
distillery
stationery (writing paper)

Here's a fun little bunny: Both *confectionery* and *confectionary* are correct. The first spelling is preferred, however.

Therefore, if you have to guess, the big money's on *–ary* as opposed to *–ery*.

Drive It On Home

Add the missing *ie/ei* to each of these words.

1. w __________ rd
2. s __________ ze
3. n __________ ghbor
4. forf __________ t
5. dec __________ ve
6. c __________ ling

Spell each of the following words correctly. Then cite the rule that you used.

7. superseed ______________________
8. healthfull ______________________
9. exced ______________________
10. mirthfuly ______________________

Answers:

1. weird
2. seize
3. neighbor
4. forfeit
5. deceive
6. ceiling
7. supersede (This is the only English verb that ends in –*sede*.)
8. healthful (At the end of a word, *full* is spelled with only one *l*.)
9. exceed (There are only three verbs in English that end in –*ceed* . . . and this is one of them.)
10. mirthfully (When the suffix is –*ful* plus –*ly*, there are two *l*'s.)

More Rules!

Q is Followed by *U*

This is a nice rule, because it has only one English exception, the lightweight nylon fabric called *Qiana.* As you can imagine, this word tends not to come up much in writing (or anywhere, for that matter). *Quarter, quality,* and *equality* all fit the rule so nicely. Here are some more *q* words you can depend on:

quartz	quota
quack	qualification
quadrant	quadriceps
quilt	question
quotation	quickly

The rule doesn't fit with abbreviations or foreign words, however. For instance, the abbreviation for *quart* is *qt.* (not *qut.*) The east Arabia peninsula on the Persian Gulf is *Qatar,* not *Quatar,* but that's okay, because the word can also be spelled "Katar." For ordinary English words however, the *qu* rule is as dependable as death and taxes.

K's and *C*'s

You know it's important to mind your *p*'s and *q*'s, but did you know that as far as spelling is concerned, you're better off on the lookout for those *k*'s and *c*'s. Some words that end in *c* have a hard "k" sound. Adding *y, i,* or *e* after the final *c* changes the hard sound to a soft one, creating spelling dilemmas. As a general rule, add a *k* after the final *c* when the hard sound becomes soft. Here are some examples:

K's and C's

Word Ending in C	Adding the K
picnic	picnicked, picnicking, picnicker
mimic	mimicked, mimicking, mimicker
politic	politicking
traffic	trafficked, trafficking, trafficker
panic	panicked, panicking, panicky

Drive It On Home

Using the rules you've learned so far in this chapter, spell each of the following words correctly. Cite the rule next to each word.

1. qagmire ____________ ____________
2. mimiced ____________ ____________
3. qisling ____________ ____________
4. picniced ____________ ____________
5. qadriceps ____________ ____________
6. panicing ____________ ____________
7. qota ____________ ____________
8. trafficer ____________ ____________
9. qotidian ____________ ____________
10. politicing ____________ ____________

Answers:

1. quagmire—*q* is followed by *u*
2. mimicked—add a *k* after the final *c* when the hard sound becomes soft
3. quisling—*q* is followed by *u*
4. picnicked—add a *k* after the final *c* when the hard sound becomes soft
5. quadriceps—*q* is followed by *u*
6. panicking—add a *k* after the final *c* when the hard sound becomes soft
7. quota—*q* is followed by *u*
8. trafficker—add a *k* after the final *c* when the hard sound becomes soft
9. quotidian—*q* is followed by *u*
10. politicking—add a *k* after the final *c* when the hard sound becomes soft

The Sahara ~~Dessert~~ Desert

Some pairs or groups of words are often mixed up with each other. Sometimes it is because the words sound alike; other times it is because they are spelled alike but carry different meanings. In either event, distinguishing between these confusing words is crucial for writing what you really mean. Keeping these partners in crime straight can also save you from some embarrassing mistakes.

The prime offenders are called *homonyms* and *homophones. Homonyms* are words with the same spelling and pronunciations but different meanings, such as *bay/bay* and *beam/beam. Homophones* are words with the same pronunciation but different spellings and meanings, such as *coarse/course* or *bridal/bridle.* In general, homophones are more commonplace than homonyms.

SMARTY PANTS

A *pallet* is a crude bed; a *palette* is an artist's paint-daub holder.

A ~~Peace~~ Piece of the Action

Now it's time to bite the bullet and learn to distinguish these words from their buddies. Here are twenty-five of the worst offenders:

1.	*air*: atmosphere	There's no air in a vacuum.
	err: make a mistake	To err is human; to purr, feline.
2.	*a lot:* many	We have a lot of time.
	allot: divide	Allot the Ping-Pong balls equally, please.
3.	*allowed*: given permission	Democracy is being allowed to vote for the candidate you dislike least.
	aloud: out loud, verbally	Don't say it aloud.
4.	*are:* plural verb	Mae West said, "Brains are an asset, if you hide them."
	our: belonging to us	Where is our car?
5.	*bore*: tiresome person	A bore is someone who, when you ask him how he is, tells you.
	boar: male pig	The farmer had a boar, cows, and chickens.
6.	*buy:* to purchase	Buy high, sell low.
	by: near or next to	Place the cookies by the milk.
7.	*cent:* a penny	I don't have a cent left.
	scent: aroma	The perfume has a sweet scent.
8.	*cheep:* what a bird says	"Cheep," said the canary.
	cheap: not expensive	Talk is cheap because supply exceeds demand.

9. *deer*: animal — The deer sneered at the inept hunter.
   dear: beloved — Dear Sweetcheeks,
10. *do*: act or make (verb) — Do your best.
    due: caused by (adjective) — Due to the storm, the picnic is canceled.
11. *fare*: transportation fee — The bus fare is $1.25.
    fair: not biased; good — The teacher is a fair grader.
12. *gorilla*: ape — King Kong is a gorilla.
    guerrilla: soldier — The guerrilla is armed to the teeth.
13. *hair:* the stuff on your head — Ken has blond hair.
    heir: beneficiary — The heirs inherited a lot of money.
14. *here*: in this place — Put the bread here.
    hear: listen — Do you hear the noise?
15. *it's:* contraction for "it is" — It's a nice day for a swim.
    its: possessive pronoun — The dog wagged its tail.
16. *lay:* to put down — Lay your cards down, partner.
    lie: be flat; untruth — Lie down if you are sick.
17. *lead:* to conduct; bluish-gray metal — The vault is lined in lead.
    led: past tense of "to lead" — The dogs led the detectives to the bone.
18. *meat*: animal flesh — We had meat for dinner.
    meet: encounter; proper — Meet me in St. Louis.
19. *peace*: calm — The peace treaty was signed.
    piece: section — Have a piece of pie.
20. *plain*: not beautiful; obvious; land mass — It's as plain as the nose on your face.
    plane: airplane — The plane is late.

	Word	Example
21.	*principal*: main; head of a school	Ms. Fink is the school's principal.
	principle: rule	Newton's principle of motion.
22.	*than*: comparison	A Great Dane is bigger than a poodle.
	then: at that time	Can you meet us then?
23.	*their*: belonging to them	It is their car.
	they're: contraction for "they are"	They're pleased with it.
	there: place	Sit over there.
24.	*weather:* atmospheric conditions	The weather is clear.
	whether: if	We're in the game, whether or not they are.
25.	*you're:* you are	You're my buddy.
	your: belonging to you	That's your fault.

Drive It On Home

Choose the correct word or words in each sentence. Warning: I included some that I didn't mention in the previous list. (Hey, why not get the extra practice?)

1. The secret of staying young is (too, two, to) live honestly, eat slowly, and (lie, lay) about (you're, your) age.
2. What did the mother broom say to the baby broom? (Its, It's) time to go to sweep.

3. A Los Angeles man, who later said he was "tired of walking," stole a steamroller and (lead, led) police on a 5 mph chase until an officer stepped aboard and brought the vehicle to a stop.
4. What (lays, lies) on (it's, its) back, (won, one) hundred feet in the (err, air)? A dead centipede.
5. Once at a social gathering, Gladstone said to Disraeli: "I predict, sir, that you will (dye, die) (buy, by) hanging or of some (vile, vial) disease." Disraeli replied, "That all depends, sir, upon (whether, weather) I embrace (you're, your) (principals, principles) or (you're, your) mistress."
6. A louse in the cabbage is better (then, than) (know, no) (meet, meat) at all.
7. (It's, Its) lonely at the top, but you eat better (they're, there).
8. What is the best thing to do if you find a (guerrilla, gorilla) in (you're, your) bed? Sleep somewhere else.
9. (To, Too, Two) bad the only people who (no, know) how to run the country (our, are) busy driving cabs and cutting (hair, heir).
10. We (our, are) (hear, here) on Earth to do good (four, for) others.
11. (Piece, Peace): In international affairs, a period of cheating between (to, too, two) periods of fighting.
12. Cats (are, our) intended to teach us that not everything in nature has a function.
13. My date was such a (boar, bore) that he put even himself to sleep.
14. Upon hearing that Ronald Reagan had been elected governor of California, movie studio head Jack Warner said, "(It's, Its) (our, are) fault. We should have given him better parts."
15. What kind of eggs does a wicked chicken (lie, lay)? Deviled eggs.

SMARTY PANTS

A *leech* is a bloodsucking worm (not a lawyer, as is rumored); to *leach* is to dissolve through percolation.

ANSWERS:

1. The secret of staying young is to live honestly, eat slowly, and lie about your age.
2. What did the mother broom say to the baby broom? It's time to go to sweep.

3. A Los Angeles man, who later said he was "tired of walking," stole a steamroller and led police on a 5 mph chase until an officer stepped aboard and brought the vehicle to a stop.

4. What lies on its back, one hundred feet in the air? A dead centipede.
5. Once at a social gathering, Gladstone said to Disraeli: "I predict, sir, that you will die by hanging or of some vile disease." Disraeli replied, "That all depends, sir, upon whether I embrace your principles or your mistress."

6. A louse in the cabbage is better than no meat at all.

7. It's lonely at the top, but you eat better there.
8. What is the best thing to do if you find a gorilla in your bed? Sleep somewhere else.

9. Too bad the only people who know how to run the country are busy driving cabs and cutting hair.

10. We are here on earth to do good for others.
11. Peace: In international affairs, a period of cheating between two periods of fighting.

12. Cats are intended to teach us that not everything in nature has a function.

13. My date was such a bore that he put even himself to sleep.
14. Upon hearing that Ronald Reagan had been elected governor of California, movie studio head Jack Warner said, “It’s our fault. We should have given him better parts.”
15. What kind of eggs does a wicked chicken lay? Deviled eggs.

Smarty Pants

A *hangar* is an airplane garage; a *hanger* is a wire implement for hanging clothing in a closet.

Chapter 9

Why Can't a PRONOUN *Be More Like a* NOUN?

(or Help Me Hurt You, Part 1)

Ever mutter to yourself: "Well, even if I *did* speak perfect English, to whom would I speak it?" Okay, so you've never said this. Work with me here.

When we speak, it's often in casual situations, so no one's watching your "who's" and "whom's." But when you speak and write in formal situations, the "who's" and "whom's" *really* matter. So do all those other pesky pronouns.

In this chapter, I'll make *who, whom,* and all the other pronouns so simple that you'll wonder what all the fuss is about. (Actually, I'm taking credit where it's really not due. That's because pronouns aren't really that difficult to begin with.)

Case Law

You learned in Chapter 2 that pronouns take the place of nouns. You also learned that there are different kinds of pronouns, based on their function in a sentence.

Case is the fancy word for the form of a noun or pronoun that shows how it is used in a sentence. Thus, *case* is the grammatical role that a noun or pronoun plays in a sentence. English has three cases: *nominative*, *objective*, and *possessive*. The following chart shows the pronouns and their form in the three cases.

The Three Cases

Nominative	Objective	Possessive
I	me	my, mine
you	you	your, yours
he	him	his
she	her	her, hers
it	it	its
we	us	our, ours
they	them	their, theirs
who	whom	whose
whoever	whomever	whoever

Nominative case

In the nominative case, the pronoun is used as a subject of a verb or a predicate nominative. This means that the pronoun *does* the action. Here are some examples:

Pronoun as the Subject of the Verb:

Who goes there?

"Who" is the subject of the verb "goes."

She planned to go to the rave.

"She" is the subject of the verb "planned."

I do most of the cooking.

"I" is the subject of the verb "cooking."

Pronoun as Predicate Nominative:

The *predicate nominative* is the noun or pronoun that follows a linking verb. It identifies or renames the subject.

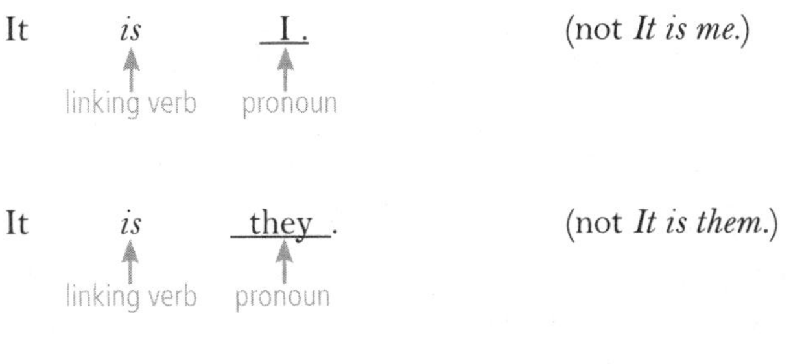

Drive It On Home

Circle the correct pronoun or pronouns in each sentence.

1. Ever wonder about those people (whom, who) spend $2 apiece on those little bottles of Evian water? Try spelling Evian backwards: NAIVE.
2. What hair color do (them, they) put on the driver's licenses of bald men?
3. Why do they put pictures of criminals up in the Post Office? What are (we, us) supposed to do, write to (they, them)?
4. If it's true that (us, we) are here to help others, then what exactly are (they, them) here for?
5. Gene and (I, me) bought lottery tickets.
6. (Us, We) boys want to hit it big.
7. The clerk said, "The winner is (him, you)!
8. (I, me) can't wait to collect my prize.
9. (He, Him) has been my lucky charm for years.
10. (Me, I) was playing golf. I swung, missed the ball, and got a big chunk of dirt. I swung again, missed the ball, and got another big chunk of dirt. Just then, two ants climbed on the ball saying, "Let (we, us) get up here before (us, we) get killed!"

Answers:

1. who	2. they	3. we, them	4. we, they
5. I	6. We	7. you	8. I
9. He	10. I, us, we		

Objective Case

In the objective case, the pronoun is used as a direct object, indirect object, or object of a preposition. The pronoun *receives* the action.

Pronoun as Direct Object:

The messy house pleased me. (not *I*)

The thunderstorm frightened the dog and them. (not *they*)

Pronoun as Indirect Object:

The sushi gave us a buzz.

My sister sent me a stud from Paris.

Pronoun as the Object of a Preposition:

Sit *by* me.

preposition pronoun

I refuse to speak *to* her.

preposition pronoun

Drive It On Home

Circle the correct pronoun in each sentence.

1. I was thinking about how people seem to read the Bible a whole lot more as they get older; then it dawned on (I, me). . . . They are cramming for their final exam.
2. Why don't they just put pictures of criminals on postage stamps so the mailmen can look for (they, them) while (them, they) deliver the mail?
3. Some people are alive only because it's illegal to kill (they, them).
4. Give (I, me) ambiguity or give (I, me) something else.
5. A doctor has a stethoscope on a man's chest. The man asks, "Doc, how do I stand?" The doctor says, "That's what puzzles (I, me)!"
6. Give (she, her) and (they, them) a noogie, please.
7. My horse's jockey was hitting the horse. The horse turns around and says, "Why are you hitting me; there is nobody behind (we, us)!"
8. Patient: "Doctor, you've got to do something to help (I, me). I snore so loudly that I keep waking myself up." Doctor: "In that case, sleep in another room."
9. My sister sent my brother and (I, me) a knuckle sandwich.
10. My mother often complains about (we, us).

Answers:

1. me
2. them, they
3. them
4. me, me
5. me
6. her, them
7. us
8. me
9. me
10. us

Possessive Case

In the possessive case, the pronoun is used to show ownership. This means that the pronoun owns something. Possessive pronouns can be used before nouns or alone.

Mark left <u>his</u> scarf at the club.
possessive pronoun

Do you mind <u>my</u> borrowing your other one?
possessive pronoun

The machete is <u>mine</u>, not <u>yours</u>.
possessive pronoun possessive pronoun

Drive It On Home

Circle the correct pronoun in each sentence.

1. If a cow laughs, would milk come out of (she, her, hers) nose?
2. A stupid guy locked his keys in the car. It took an hour to get (he, his) wife out.
3. Why were the teacher's eyes crossed? She couldn't control (she, her, her's) pupils.
4. May (you're, your) sports utility vehicle hold (it's, its) resale value.
5. You can't trust dogs to watch (your, you're) food.
6. (His, Him) constant smile depressed (we, us) all.
7. I tried sniffing Coke once, but the ice cubes got stuck in (me, my) nose.

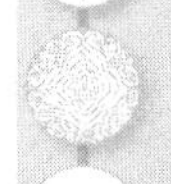

8. I thought you would really understand (our, us) practical joking.
9. It's always darkest just before I open (me, my) eyes.
10. Why do psychics have to ask you for (you're, your) name?

Answers:

1. her	2. his	3. her	4. your, its
5. your	6. His, us	7. my	8. our
9. my	10. your		

Drive It On Home

Work it, baby. Choose the correct pronoun and identify the case.

1. Bob and (I, me) decided to go to Ho-Ho-Kus on vacation.

   ____

2. Valencia gave (her, she) a lot of unsolicited advice.

   ____

3. I spoke to him about (his, him) comb-over.

   ____

4. The leaders are Reggie and (she, her).

   ____

5. This is between you and (I, me), so don't get them involved.

   ____

Smarty Pants

In compound structures (those with two pronouns or a noun and a pronoun), drop the other word for the moment. Then you can see which case you need. For example:

Bob and (I, me) travel a lot.   I travel a lot.

This tells you the answer is "I," the nominative case.

6. My father and (me, I) installed the air conditioner.

____

7. (Your, You) leaving will be a relief, frankly.

____

8. My landlord lent (I, me) his power tools.

____

9. The culprits are (them, they).

____

10. I congratulated (she, her) on the raise.

____

Answers:

1. I (nominative)
2. her (indirect object)
3. his (possessive)
4. she (predicate nominative)
5. me (object of the preposition "between")
6. I (nominative)
7. Your (possessive)
8. me (indirect object)
9. they (predicate nominative)
10. her (direct object)

On the Case with Who and Whom

No doubt *who* and *whom* drive more people mad than all other grammar issues put together. Either that, or *who* and *whom* are just more visible and bothered your eighth-grade English teacher more than the gum-chewing tarts in the back row. In either event, let's solve this burning issue so we can worry about the really important things, like what you should wear to your high school reunion and whether it's really worth it to rent a Rolls for the event. (Wear black and yes, the car is worth it.)

The following charts lay it all out.

The Singular Forms of Who/Whom

Nominative	Objective	Possessive
who	whom	whose
whoever	whomever	whosever

The Plural Forms of Who/Whom

Nominative	Objective	Possessive
who	whom	whose
whoever	whomever	whosever

Fortunately, you get a break: The singular and plural forms of *who* and *whoever* are the same. Even better, *who* and *whom* are used the same as the personal pronouns we just discussed, as the following chart reinforces:

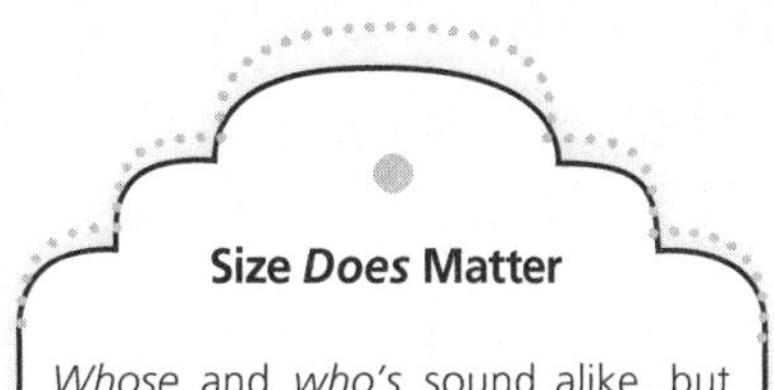

Size *Does* Matter

Whose and *who's* sound alike, but that's where the resemblance ends. *Whose* is a pronoun; *who's* is a contraction meaning "who is."

Who/Whom and the Three Cases

Nominative	Objective	Possessive
who	whom	whose
whoever	whomever	whosever

Nominative Case

Since *who* is nothing more than a pronoun in a scary mask, it's used just like any other pronoun in the nominative case.

Who as the Subject of the Verb:

Who won the football pool this week?

I know who barfed on my shoes.

Who as Predicate Nominative:

The winner *was* who?
(linking verb: *was*; pronoun: who)

No one knew *who* the winner was.
(pronoun: *who*; linking verb: was)

Smarty Pants

Remember that *who* follows the same pattern as "he/they." *Whom* follows the same pattern as "him, them." When all three words are in the objective case, they end with *m*: who*m*, hi*m*, the*m*.

Objective Case

Whom and *whomever* are the babies that take off in the objective case, as these examples show.

Pronoun as Direct Object:

Whom did she finally marry?

object subject

Naturally, she can marry whomever she wants.

subject object

Pronoun as Object of a Preposition:

With whom were you French-kissing?

preposition pronoun

We are excited to meet the kisser *about* whom we have heard so much.

preposition pronoun

Smarty Pants

Remember this John Donne quote to help keep who/whom straight: "Don't ask for whom the bell tolls; it tolls for thee."

Drive It On Home

Circle the correct pronoun in each sentence. Then explain if the pronoun is in the nominative, objective, or possessive case.

1. From (who, whom) did you get that dreadful dog?
2. (Who, Whom) is the designated driver?
3. (Whose, Who's) car are we using tonight?
4. The group chose (who, whom)?
5. (Who, Whom) at the party knows how to cook a turkey?
6. With (whom, who) have you decided to attend the party?
7. (Whose, Who's) clothes should we borrow for the vacation?
8. (Whoever, Whomever) is hired will get the short end of the stick, like the rest of us.
9. Tell (whoever, whomever) you wish about my decision to pierce my bellybutton.
10. Share the cookies with (whoever, whomever) asks for some.

Answers:

1. whom (objective case, object of the pronoun "from")
2. Who (nominative case)
3. Whose (possessive case)
4. whom (objective case)
5. Who (nominative case)
6. whom (objective case, object of the pronoun "with")
7. Whose (possessive case)
8. Whoever (nominative case)
9. whomever (objective case, direct object)
10. whoever (nominative case)

Drive It On Home

Circle the correct pronouns in the following anecdote.

Mrs. Pete Monaghan came into the newsroom to pay for (hers, her) husband's obituary. The kindly newsman told (she, her) that it cost $1 a word, and he said he remembered Pete and wasn't it too bad about (his, him) passing away. She thanked (he, him) for (his, he's) kind words and bemoaned the fact that she only had $2. But she wrote out the obituary, "Pete died."

The newsman said he thought someone like Pete (who, whom) died deserved more. "He was a man (whom, who) everyone liked," he said, so he'd give (she, her) three more words at no charge. Mrs. Monaghan thanked him and rewrote the obituary: "Pete died. Boat for sale."

Answer:

Mrs. Pete Monaghan came into the newsroom to pay for her husband's obituary. The kindly newsman told her that it cost $1 a word, and he said he remembered Pete and wasn't it too bad about his passing away. She thanked him for his kind words and bemoaned the fact that she only had $2. But she wrote out the obituary, "Pete died."

The newsman said he thought someone like Pete <u>who</u> died deserved more. "He was a man <u>whom</u> everyone liked," he said, so he'd give <u>her</u> three more words at no charge. Mrs. Monaghan thanked him and rewrote the obituary: "Pete died. Boat for sale."

Chapter 10

Four Play: *Four Common* GRAMMAR *Headaches*

What's wrong with the following four sentences?

1. Our new car were all scratched up.
2. This is the most worse thing that ever happened!
3. Do not sit on the swing set without being assembled.
4. Take the bull by the potholders.

They're all head scratchers, eh? You know they sound wrong, but perhaps you can't figure out why. Each one contains a grammatical error. The envelope, please.

1. The first sentence has an error in agreement of subject and verb. The correct sentence reads: Our new car *was* all scratched up.

2. The second sentence has a problem with the comparative form. It should read: This is the *worst* thing that ever happened!
3. The third sentence is a dangling modifier. As the sentence reads, it means that the person—not the swing set—isn't fully assembled. This is possible, but not likely. The correct sentence should read: Do not sit on the swing set *until it is* assembled.
4. And the last sentence? It's a mixed metaphor. That means the comparison isn't between related things. The comparison should read: Take the bull by the *horns*.

This chapter covers these four common and annoying grammar errors. Each of these problems can make it difficult for your audience to understand what you're saying and writing, so we'll banish them now.

A Match Made in Heaven: Agreement of Subject and Verb

When you match your clothing, you coordinate colors and fabrics. When you match sentence parts, you coordinate number—singular and plural. Remember that *singular* means "one" and *plural* means "more than one." *Agreement* is just the fancy-schmancy grammar word for "matching." Here's the easy rule:

A subject must agree with its verb in number.

Now for some explanation and examples.

The Process

Follow these steps to check for agreement:

1. Find the subject in the sentence. Remember that the subject will be a noun or a pronoun.
2. Determine whether the subject is singular or plural.
3. Figure out which form of the verb is singular and which form is plural. Pick the one that matches the subject.

The following charts show some singular and plural nouns/pronouns and verbs.

Singular and Plural Nouns and Pronouns

Singular	Plural
toy	toys
egg	eggs
inch	inches
man	men
dog	dogs
ox	oxen
each	others
one	several

Singular and Plural Verbs in the Present Tense

First and Second Person Singular	Third Person Singular	First, Second, and Third Person Plural
(I, you) start	(he, she, it) starts	(we, you, they) start
(I, you) do	(he, she, it) does	(we, you, they) do

Drive It On Home

Label each of the following words as "noun," "pronoun," or "verb." Then label them as "singular" or "plural."

1. is
2. felines
3. several
4. goes
5. make
6. sleeps
7. grow
8. oceans
9. anybody
10. were

Answers:

1. verb, singular
2. noun, plural
3. pronoun, plural
4. verb, singular
5. verb, plural
6. verb, singular
7. verb, plural
8. noun, plural
9. pronoun, singular
10. verb, plural

Singular Subject = Singular Verb

You've already learned that *a subject must agree with its verb in number.* A singular subject requires a singular verb. This is true of pronouns as well as nouns. Here are some examples:

The sex was so good that even the neighbors had a cigarette.
singular subject singular verb

Peanut butter and jelly is my favorite sandwich.
singular subject singular verb
(functions as one unit)

The Joy of Sex has found a home on many bookshelves.
singular subject singular verb
(titles are always singular)

Plural Subject = Plural Verb

A plural subject takes a plural verb. This is true of pronouns as well as nouns. Here are some examples:

Do Lipton Tea employees take coffee breaks?
plural subject plural verb

How do dinosaurs pay their bills? With Tyrannosaurus checks.
plural subject plural verb

My sister and my brother are late, as usual.
plural subject plural verb

(two singular subjects joined by "and" = a plural subject)

Show and Tell

Think of the conjunction "and" as a plus sign. Whether the parts of the subject joined by "and" are singular or plural (or both), they all add up to a plural subject and so require a plural verb.

Drive It On Home

Choose the correct verb to complete each sentence.

1. Bessie Braddock, an outspoken political opponent of Winston Churchill, told him one day, "Winston, you (is, are) drunk." He immediately replied, "Bessie, you (is, are) ugly. And tomorrow morning I shall be sober."
2. Churchill and George Bernard Shaw also crossed swords. According to the legend, Shaw sent Churchill two tickets for the first night of his play with a note saying, "Bring a friend, if you (has, have) one." Churchill returned the tickets, saying he could not attend but would be grateful for tickets to the second night, "if there (is, are) one."
3. Politician Adlai Stevenson once said, "Man (does, do) not live by words alone, despite the fact that sometimes he (has, have) to eat them."
4. Oscar Wilde said, "Experience (is, are) the name everyone (gives, give) to their mistakes."
5. "A lower voter turnout (is, are) an indication of fewer people going to the polls." (George W. Bush or Dan Quayle)
6. "Laugh and the world (laugh, laughs) with you. Cry and you (cries, cry) with your girlfriends." (Laurie Kuslansky)
7. Oscar Wilde said, "A cynic is a man who (know, knows) the price of everything and the value of nothing."

8. Told that Clare Boothe Luce was kind to her inferiors, Dorothy Parker remarked, "Where (does, do) she (find, finds) them?"
9. "I (is, am) not going to vacuum until Sears (make, makes) one you can ride on." (Roseanne Barr)
10. On the wall in a ladies' room: "My husband (follow, follows) me everywhere." Written just below it: "I (do, does) not."

Answers:

1. are, are
2. have, is
3. does, has
4. is, gives
5. is
6. laughs, cry
7. knows
8. does, find
9. am, makes
10. follows, do

Special Cases

If the subject is made up of two or more nouns or pronouns connected by *or, nor, not only,* or *but also,* the verb agrees with the noun closer to the pronoun.

My sister *or* my brothers (plural subject) have (plural verb) bought the flowers.

My brothers *or* my sister (singular subject) has (singular verb) bought the flowers.

Collective nouns (nouns that name groups of people or things) are singular, even if they end in *–s.* That's because they function as one unit. Here are some collective nouns: *jury, committee, team, class, audience, flock, group, club, assembly.* And some examples:

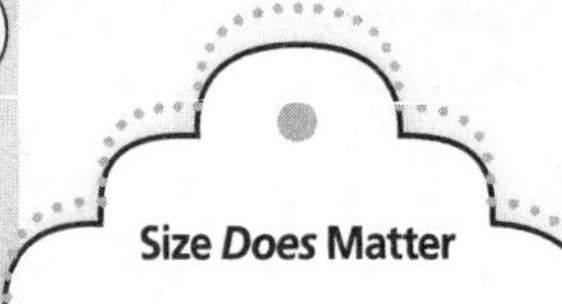

Size *Does* Matter

Ignore words or phrases that come between the subject and the verb. A phrase or clause that comes between a subject and its verb does not affect subject-verb agreement. For example: The captain of the guards stands at attention.

The committee has made its decision.
singular subject singular verb

The class is unusually obstreperous today.
singular subject singular verb

Don't be fooled by plural-looking subjects like *measles*, *news*, *mathematics*, and *social studies*. They're still singular, even though they end in –*s*.

The news was good
singular subject singular verb

Economics is called the "dismal science."
singular subject singular verb

Pronouns and Agreement

As with nouns and verbs, pronouns must match the words to which they refer—their antecedents. Here's the rule: *A personal pronoun must agree with its antecedent in number, person, and gender.*

Remember that an *antecedent* is the noun or group of words acting as a noun that the pronoun stands for. The antecedent usually comes before the pronoun but it can follow it as well.

The following chart explains all this "number, person, gender" stuff.

Three-Way Trysts

Number	**Person**	**Gender**
singular or plural	first person (I, me, my, mine, we, us, our, ours) or second person (you, your, yours) or third person (he, him, his, she, her, hers, it, its, they, them, their, theirs)	masculine (he), feminine (she), or neuter (it)

And here are some examples:

Don't Agree in Number:

Ben and Jerry have changed his plans for Cherry Garcia.

plural antecedent — singular personal pronoun

Do agree in number:

Ben and Jerry have changed their plans for Cherry Garcia.

plural antecedent — plural personal pronoun

Don't Agree in Number:

Neither Thelma nor Louise can find their half gallon of Chunky Monkey.

singular antecedent — plural personal pronoun

(two singular antecedents joined by *or* or *nor* are singular.)

Do Agree in Number:

Neither Thelma nor Louise can find her half gallon of Chunky Monkey.

singular antecedent — singular personal pronoun

(two singular antecedents joined by *or* or *nor* are singular.)

Don't Agree in Person:

Jill is studying underwater fire prevention, a course you needs to graduate.

feminine antecedent — second-person pronoun

Do Agree in Person:

Jill is studying underwater fire prevention, a course she needs to graduate.

feminine antecedent — feminine personal pronoun

Don't Agree in Gender:

Each nation has its own culture and our nation has his culture, too.

nation: neuter antecedent; its: neuter pronoun; our: neuter antecedent; his: masculine pronoun

Do Agree in Gender:

Each nation has its own culture and our nation has its culture, too.

nation: neuter antecedent; its: neuter pronoun; our: neuter antecedent; its: neuter pronoun

Smarty Pants

In life, *gender* refers to the naughty bits. In grammar, *gender* means that the word is masculine (he), feminine (she), or neutral (it). Usually the word is a pronoun, but we have a few nouns that have gender links, like "pretty" for women and "macho" for men.

Indefinite Pronouns and Agreement

Indefinite pronouns refer to people, places, objects, or things without pointing to a specific one. *Indefinite pronouns* can be singular or plural, depending on how they are used in a sentence. Singular indefinite pronouns take a singular verb; plural indefinite pronouns take a plural verb.

Indefinite pronouns that end in *–one* or *–body* are always singular. For example: *anyone, everyone, someone, one, anybody, somebody, nobody.* The indefinite pronouns *both, few, many, others,* and *several* are always plural. The indefinite pronouns *all, any, more, most, none,* and *some* can be singular or plural, depending on how they are used. Here are some examples:

One of my boots is missing.
singular subject — singular verb

Both of my boots are missing.
plural subject — plural verb

All the soup was eaten
singular subject — singular verb

All the seats were taken.
plural subject — plural verb

Drive It On Home

Choose the correct verb or verbs to complete each sentence.

1. If FedEx and UPS (was, were) to merge, would they call the company Fed UP?
2. Neither of the boys has received (his, their) grades yet.
3. Both my parents sent (her, his, their) checks.
4. Several of the cars had (his, their) bumpers smashed.
5. We returned each of the shoes to (their, its) proper box.
6. Neither Rita nor Nicole can find (their, her) watch.
7. What do you call a dinosaur that smashes everything in (their, its) path? Tyrannosaurus wrecks.
8. What do you call a country where everyone (have, has) to drive a red car? A red carnation.
9. Chuck is eating spinach, a vegetable (he, you, we) needs to stay healthy.
10. Employees should buy (his, her, their) Girl Scout cookies from Shelby.

Answers:

1. were	2. his	3. their	4. their
5. its	6. her	7. its	8. has
9. he	10. their		

Third Degree: Comparing with Adjectives and Adverbs

Adjectives and adverbs have different forms to show degree of comparison. We even have a name for each of these forms of degree: *positive*, *comparative*, and *superlative*. Here they are:

- *Positive degree:* the base form of the adjective or adverb. It does not show comparison.
- *Comparative degree:* the form an adjective or adverb takes to compare *two* things.
- *Superlative degree:* the form an adjective or adverb takes to compare *three* things.

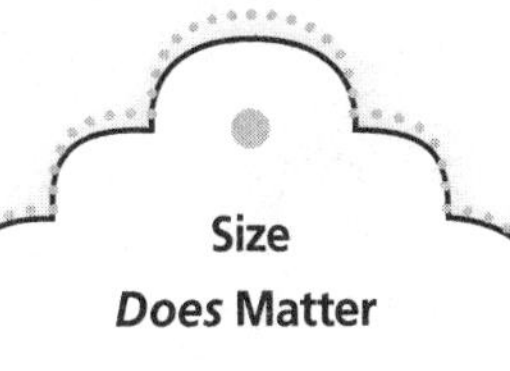

Size *Does* Matter

Make sure that you compare only items of similar kind. Here are two comparisons that do not work: "She was as easy as the *TV Guide* crossword puzzle" and "'Oh Jason, take me,' she panted, her breasts heaving like a college freshman on $1-a-beer night."

The following chart shows the three degrees of comparison with some sample adjectives and adverbs.

You Should Have Seen the Size of the One That Got Away

	Positive	Comparative	Superlative
adjectives	tall	taller	tallest
	good	better	best
adverbs	slowly	more slowly	most slowly
	well	better	best

Let's review the rules for forming the comparative and superlative degrees. (These *will* seem familiar to you, I promise.)

1. To form the comparative degree, add *–er* or *more* (NEVER both!) to most one- and two-syllable adjectives and adverbs. To form the superlative degree, add *–est* or *most* (NEVER both!) to most one- and two-syllable adjectives and adverbs. Most of the time, we add *–er* or *–est*, but *more* and *most* can also be used. Use the form that sounds best. Here are some examples:

   weak . . . . weaker . . . . weakest
   strong . . . . stronger. . . . . strongest
   frail . . . . more frail . . . . most frail
   honest . . . . more honest . . . . most honest

2. Use *more* or *most* to form the comparative and superlative degrees of all adjectives and adverbs that have three or more syllables. Here are some examples:

   extensive. . . . . . more extensive . . . . . most extensive
   prevalent. . . . . . more prevalent . . . . . most prevalent

3. Use *more* and *most* with all adverbs that end in *–ly.* Here are some examples:

   easily. . . . . more easily . . . . most easily
   rudely . . . . more rudely. . . . . most rudely
   nicely. . . . . more nicely . . . . most nicely

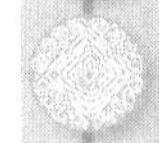

Irregular Adjectives and Adverbs

Of course, there's always a spoilsport. In this case, we have a few adjectives and adverbs that don't follow these rules. Naturally, these are among the most common adjectives and adverbs we use. Go figure.

The following chart shows the most common irregular adjectives and adverbs.

Cranky Adjectives and Adverbs

Positive	Comparative	Superlative
good	better	best
well	better	best
bad	worse	worst
badly	worse	worst
far	farther	farthest
far	further	furthest
late	later	later or latest
little (amount)	less	least
many	more	most
much	more	most
some	more	most

Smarty Pants

When you compare one of a group with the rest of the group, make sure that your sentence contains the word *other* or *else*. For example: Roosevelt was greater than any *other* president.

Drive It On Home

Choose the correct word to complete each sentence.

1. "There is only one thing in the world (worst, worse) than being talked about, and that is not being talked about." (Oscar Wilde)
2. "The future will be (gooder, more good, better) tomorrow." (George W. Bush or Dan Quayle)
3. "We are going to have the (better, best) educated American people in the world." (George W. Bush or Dan Quayle)
4. "For NASA, space is still the (high, higher, highest) priority." (George W. Bush or Danny Boy)
5. Why do old men wear their pants (high, higher, highest) than young men?
6. "Things are going to get a lot (worst, worse) before they get (worst, worse)." (Lily Tomlin)
7. He said: "Shall we try swapping positions tonight?"
   She said: "That's a (good, better, best) idea. You stand by the ironing board while I sit on the sofa."
8. Q: Why are married women (heavy, heavier, heaviest) than single women?
   A: Single women come home, see what's in the fridge, and go to bed. Married woman come home, see what's in the bed, and go to the fridge.
9. Why is it that inside every (older, oldest) person is a (younger, youngest) person wondering what the heck happened?
10. Her vocabulary was as (bad, worse, worst) as like, whatever.

Answers:

1. worse
2. better
3. best
4. highest
5. higher
6. worse, worse
7. good
8. heavier
9. older, younger
10. bad

Misplaced and Dangling Modifiers

The following inscription comes from a tombstone in Edinburgh, Scotland:

> Erected in the memory of
> John MacFarlane, Drowned in the Water of Leith
> By a few affectionate friends

Now, did the friends drown John or did they erect the tombstone in his memory? According to the tombstone, it was the former. With friends like that, who needs enemies? The tombstone *should* read:

> Erected by a few affectionate friends in the memory of
> John MacFarlane, Drowned in the Water of Leith

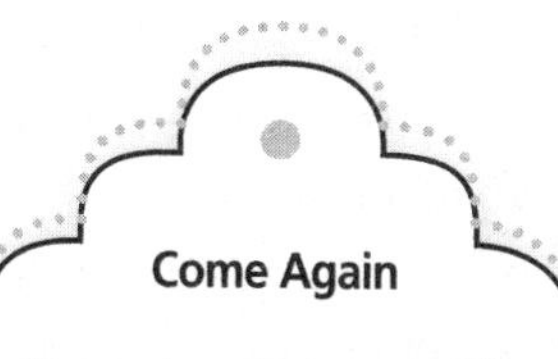

Come Again

Remember that a *modifier* is a word or phrase that gives more information about the subject, verb, or object in a clause.

The mistake in the inscription is a *misplaced modifier*, a phrase, clause, or word placed too far from the noun or pronoun it describes. As a result, the sentence fails to convey its exact meaning and can also be unintentionally funny.

Correct a misplaced modifier by placing it in the correct place in the sentence. Here are two more examples.

Misplaced: Coming in for a landing, ground control radioed to the helicopter.
(states that ground control is coming in for a landing)
Corrected: Ground control radioed to the helicopter coming in for a landing,

Misplaced: Smashed beyond repair, Larry saw his tennis racket lying on the court.
(states that Larry is smashed)
Corrected: Larry saw his tennis racket, smashed beyond repair, lying on the court.

A *dangling modifier* is a word or phrase that describes something that has been left out of the sentence. A modifier is said to "dangle" when the word it modifies (describes) is not actually in the sentence.

Correct a dangling modifier by adding a noun or pronoun to which the dangling construction can be attached. Here are two examples.

Dangling: Flying over the countryside, the houses looked like toys.
(states that the houses were flying)
Corrected: As they were flying over the countryside, the houses looked like toys.
(added the pronoun "they" and the helping verb "were")

Dangling: After studying hard, the test was easy.
(states that the test was doing the studying)
Corrected: After Samara studied hard, the test was easy.
(added the noun "Samara" and changed the form of "studying" to match)

Drive It On Home

Correct each of the following misplaced or dangling modifiers.

1. The house was rebuilt by the new owners destroyed in the hurricane.
2. The golfer sank the putt with the green shirt.
3. Driving through the mountains at night, the pine trees looked spooky.
4. We saved the scraps of meat for the dog that have been left on our plate.
5. To get to town fast, the freeway is best.
6. Getting up earlier than usual, the house was very quiet.
7. We saw many beautiful canyons driving through Utah.
8. Two sisters were reunited after eighteen years at the checkout counter.
9. Include your children when baking cookies.
10. The killer was sentenced to die for the second time in ten years.

Answers:

1. The house destroyed in the hurricane was rebuilt by the new owners.
2. The golfer with the green shirt sank the putt.
3. As we drove through the mountains at night, the pine trees looked spooky.
4. We saved the scraps of meat that have been left on our plate for the dog.

5. If you want to get to town fast, the freeway is best.
6. When we got up earlier than usual, the house was very quiet.
7. Driving through Utah, we saw many beautiful canyons.
8. Two sisters were reunited at the checkout counter after eighteen years.
9. Include your children when you are baking cookies.
10. For the second time in ten years, the killer was sentenced to die.

Mixed Metaphors

What's wrong with this sentence?

> The ballerina rose gracefully on pointe and extended one slender leg behind her, like a dog at a fire hydrant.

The sentence merges two images that don't go together: a graceful ballerina and a squat fire hydrant. We call this a *mixed metaphor.* A *metaphor* is a figure of speech that compares two unlike things, the more familiar thing used to compare the less familiar one. Here's the metaphor rule: Compare two things that go together.

Mixed metaphor: It was an American tradition, like fathers chasing kids around with power tools.

Effective metaphor: It was an American tradition, like Mom and apple pie.

Smarty Pants

Do you know the classic metaphor joke? "Keep your eye on the ball, your ear on the ground, your nose to the grindstone, and your shoulder to the wheel—now try to work in that position."

PART THREE

Bring It On Home

Chapter 11

Watch Your Words!

Here are a few common observations that may give you something to ponder:

1. If four out of five people *suffer* from diarrhea, does that mean that one enjoys it?
2. If people from Poland are called "Poles," why aren't people from Holland called "Holes"?
3. Why is a person who plays the piano called a "pianist" but a person who drives a racecar is not called a "racist"?
4. If a pig loses its voice, is it "disgruntled"?
5. If lawyers are "disbarred" and clergymen "defrocked," doesn't it follow that electricians can be "delighted," musicians "denoted," cowboys "deranged," models "deposed," tree surgeons "debarked," and dry cleaners "depressed"?

The precise words you choose in speech and writing matter a great deal. Words with the same basic meaning will often convey vastly different impressions. Choosing the exact words that you mean can also help keep you from inadvertently offending your readers. In this chapter, I'll show you how to find the precise word you want . . . not your second-best choice.

Big Shots

When it comes to the naughty bits, bigger *may* be better—but the jury's still out on that one. When it comes to words, the verdict is in: Bigger isn't always better. As you choose words, don't reach so quickly for the ones with many syllables. Instead, find the word that says what you mean. In all cases, *write simply and directly.* Here's your test: If a word, phrase, or statement makes you scratch your head in confusion, it's not clear writing. For example:

Alan Greenspan once testified before a Senate committee that "it is a tricky problem to find the particular calibration in timing that would be appropriate to stem the acceleration in risk premium created by falling incomes without much prematurely aborting the decline in the inflation-generated risk premium." We say, "huh?"

Or how about this statement from Secretary of Defense Donald Rumsfeld: "Reports that say that something hasn't happened are always interesting to me, because as we know, there are known knowns; there are things we know we know. We also know there are known unknowns; that is to say we know there are some things we do not know. But there are also unknown unknowns—the ones we don't know we don't know."

We say: "We don't know what you are talking about, Mr. Secretary."

Get the Write, Rite, Right Word

Start by choosing the most appropriate words for your audience and purpose. Most of all, make sure that you have chosen precisely the word that you want. Often, in their attempt to impress their audience, writers try to use the biggest word they can. Sadly, they often choose the wrong word. Here are two examples:

> Ancient Egypt was inhabited by mummies and they all wrote in hydraulics.
> Solomon had 300 wives and 700 porcupines.

In the first example, the writer means hieroglyphs. In the second example, the writer means concubines, not porcupines. These are long and difficult words, but they are the most appropriate words for the context.

Smarty Pants

The depth and precision of English have helped make it the foremost language of science, diplomacy, and international business.

Drive It On Home

Here are some mistakes that students really have made in their writing (as hard as some of them are to believe). Correct each sentence by supplying the word the writer *really* wanted. The errors are underlined.

1. The nineteenth century was a time of a great many thoughts and inventions. People stopped reproducing by hand and started reproducing by machine.

2. Charles Darwin was a naturalist who wrote *The Organ of Species.*
3. The Greeks were a highly sculptured people, and without them we wouldn't have history.
4. Socrates died from an overdose of wedlock.
5. In the Olympic games, Greeks ran races, jumped, hurled the biscuit, and threw the java.
6. Julius Caesar extinguished himself on the battlefields of Gaul.
7. Sir Francis Drake circumcised the world with a 100-foot clipper.
8. The greatest writer of the Renaissance was William Shakespeare. He wrote tragedies, dramas, and comedies, all in Islamic pentameter.
9. Delegates from the original thirteen states formed the Contented Congress.
10. Abraham Lincoln became America's greatest precedent. He freed the slaves by signing the Emasculation Proclamation.

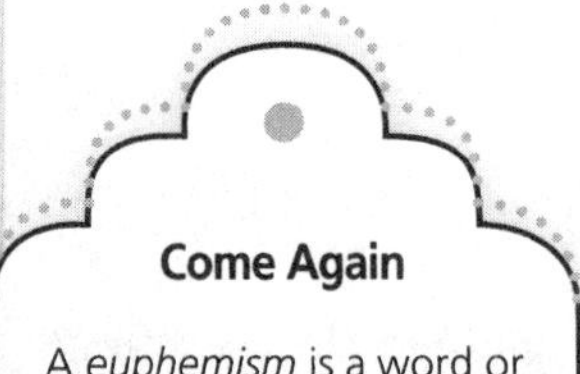

Come Again

A *euphemism* is a word or words that are designed to soften a harsh reality—for example, "servicing the target" instead of "killing the enemy."

Answers:

1. producing
2. *Origin*
3. cultured
4. hemlock
5. discus, javelin
6. distinguished
7. circumnavigated
8. iambic
9. Continental
10. president, Emancipation

Avoid "Doublespeak"

We live in an age when a "used car" or a "secondhand car" is called *pre-owned.* Bank fraud is called an *unauthorized withdrawal*; problems are called *challenges.* Being fired is called *laid-off, outplaced, downsized, rightsized, outsourced, involuntarily leisured, made redundant.* All these phrases were created to disguise or distort the writer's actual meaning. We call this type of language "doublespeak."

Smarty Pants

The word "doublespeak" was coined in the early 1950s. It is often incorrectly attributed to George Orwell in his novel *1984*. The word actually never appears in that novel; Orwell did, however, coin the terms *newspeak, oldspeak,* and *doublethink*, and his novel made composite nouns whose sole purpose was to muddle meaning fashionable.

Here are some especially egregious examples of doublespeak:

Doublespeak	**Clear Language**
collateral damage	bystander deaths
defense	war
area denial munitions	landmines
job flexibility	lack of job security

Like tongue rings and $6 cups of coffee, "doublespeak" has become pervasive today, but that doesn't make it right. Back to our motto: *Write simply and directly.*

Drive It On Home

Rewrite each of the following examples of doublespeak into understandable, honest English.

1. the Final Solution
2. vertical transportation corps
3. negative patient care outcome
4. vertically challenged
5. sanitation engineer

Sample Answers:

1. the Nazi term for killing people because they were Jewish
2. elevator operators
3. the patient died
4. short
5. garbage collector

Show and Tell

By all means use a *thesaurus* (a book of synonyms and antonyms) to find the exact word you want. A thesaurus comes in both online and print versions, but the print versions tend to have a greater selection of words than the online versions.

Undertones and Overtones: Connotation and Denotation

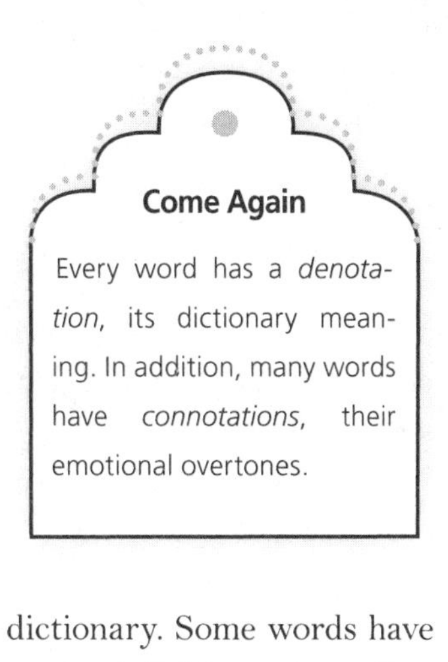
Come Again

Every word has a *denotation*, its dictionary meaning. In addition, many words have *connotations*, their emotional overtones.

Assume that you're carrying the same spare tire around your middle that we're all carrying. If so, would you rather be called *fat* or *plump*? Now assume that you're tight with a buck. In that case, would you rather be described as *stingy* or *frugal*?

Every word in every language has a *denotation*, its dictionary meaning. This is the definition you find when you look up the word in a dictionary. Some words have just one denotation, while other words may have many definitions, depending on the way they are used in a sentence. For example, the first definition for *fat* is "having too much adipose tissue; chubby, corpulent, obese." *Fat* can also mean "fertile," "prosperous," and "abundant." *Plump* is defined as "well rounded or filled out in form; somewhat fleshy or fat." As you can see, the first definitions for *fat* and *plump* are virtually identical. However, their overtones are vastly different. We call these overtones a word's *connotations.*

Fat has a negative overtone, while *plump* has a much nicer implied meaning. The same is true with *stingy* and *frugal.* Both words mean "thrifty with money." However, *stingy* is a negative character trait, while *frugal* is positive. We want to be *frugal*, not *stingy.*

As a writer looking for just the right word, you have to consider more than the word's denotation. You've got to consider each word's connotations as well to make sure that you are communicating clearly.

Writers often choose words because of their connotations as well as their denotations. For instance, Edgar Allan Poe opened a horror story about the disintegration of a family with this description: "During the whole of a dull, dark, and soundless day in the autumn of the year, when the clouds hung oppressively low in the heavens . . . " He chose the word *oppressively* because it carries the overtones of gloom, suffocation, and stuffiness. The word helps Poe create the impression of being confined and held down. Ditto on the words *dull*, *dark*, and *soundless*. Their connotations add to this feeling of gloom and doom.

A word's connotation can be positive, like the word *sprightly*, or negative, like the word *insolent*. However, remember that not all words have a connotation. For instance, the word *sound* doesn't have a connotation. The word *noise*, on the other hand, has a negative connotation of unpleasant or disturbing sound.

When you write, think carefully about the connotations as well as denotations of the words you choose.

Drive It On Home

Write *positive*, *negative*, or *neutral* to identify the connotation of each word.

1. regular	________	immaculate	________
2. frugal	________	stingy	________
3. precise	________	rigid	________
4. private	________	secretive	________
5. proud	________	conceited	________
6. mischievous	________	troublesome	________
7. intrepid	________	reckless	________

8. slender	________________	emaciated	________________
9. rowdy	________________	high-spirited	________________
10. house	________________	home	________________

Answers:

1. regular: neutral	immaculate: positive
2. frugal: positive	stingy: negative
3. precise: positive	rigid: negative
4. private: positive	secretive: negative
5. proud: positive	conceited: negative
6. mischievous: positive	troublesome: negative
7. intrepid: positive	reckless: negative
8. slender: positive	emaciated: negative
9. rowdy: negative	high-spirited: positive
10. house: neutral	home: positive

Shoot Yourself in the Foot: Biased Language

Have you heard these riddles?

> How do you make a blond's eyes twinkle? Shine a flashlight in her ear.
>
> Why did the blond keep a coat hanger in her backseat? In case she locked her keys in her car.
>
> Why did the blond get so excited after she finished her jigsaw puzzle in only six months? Because on the box it said "from two to four years."

How's about these jokes?

How many men does it take to change a roll of toilet paper? We don't know; it has never happened.

What is the difference between men and government bonds? Men mature.

Why are blond jokes so short? So men can remember them.

These silly jokes are obviously sexist and thus unacceptable. However, biased language is often far more subtle and difficult to spot. Nonetheless, it's every bit as offensive as these sexist jokes.

Biased language assigns qualities to people on the basis of their gender. It reflects stereotypical thinking and prejudiced attitudes about men and women. As a result, biased language discriminates against people by limiting what they can do. Because biased language lies and perpetuates sexist attitudes, it alienates readers. Increasingly, biased language can also cause legal problems.

Show and Tell

Because federal law forbids discrimination on the basis of gender, people who write policy statements, grant proposals, or any other official documents must avoid any language that could be considered discriminatory, especially biased language.

Use Nonbiased Language

You want to use *nonbiased language* because it treats both sexes neutrally. Follow these guidelines to help you use words truthfully and fairly when you write and speak.

1. Avoid using *man* to refer to men and women.

Biased: Although he did not go to Antarctica, Captain James Cook is generally given credit as the first man to set foot on the continent.

Not biased: Although he did not go to Antarctica, Captain James Cook is generally given credit as the first person to set foot on the continent.

2. Avoid using *he* to refer to both men and women.

   Biased: A magazine subscription and a gym membership make a good gift for the man who has everything.

   Not biased: A magazine subscription and a gym membership make a good gift for the person who has everything.

3. Avoid expressions that exclude one sex. The following list shows some of the most offensive examples and acceptable alternatives:

Biased	**Not Biased**
the common man	the average person
man-sized	huge, large
mankind	humanity
chairman	chair, chairperson
policeman	police officer
fireman	firefighter
businessman	businessperson
salesman	salesperson
waitress	server

4. Avoid language that denigrates people.

Biased: male nurse
Not biased: nurse
Biased: lady doctor
Not biased: doctor
Biased: retarded person
Not biased: mentally disabled person

5. Use the correct courtesy title.

Use *Mr.* for men and *Ms.* for women, with these two exceptions:

- In a business setting, professional titles take precedence over *Mr.* and *Ms.* For example, doctors are usually called "Dr." rather than "Ms." or "Mr."
- Always use the title the person prefers. Some women prefer "Miss" to "Ms."

Show and Tell

If you are not sure whether to use *Mrs.* or *Ms.* in a person's title, check in a company directory and on previous correspondence to see how the person prefers to be addressed. Also pay attention to the way people introduce themselves.

Drive It On Home

Replace the underlined word or words as necessary to replace biased language with nonbiased language.

1. A <u>doctor</u> shouldn't book more patients than <u>he</u> can see in a day.

2. On December 25, 1968, the *Apollo* 8 astronauts became the first men to see the far side of the moon.
3. A successful lawyer knows that he has to work long hours.
4. A man's best friend is his dog.
5. My girl will get you a cup of coffee.
6. Everyone hopes that he will win the contest.
7. The company has office gals to answer the phones.
8. No one believes that old wives' tale!
9. Everyone establishes his own "comfort zone" by seeing what he can accomplish in a specific setting.
10. Ask the stewardess for a cup of tea, please.

Sample Answers:

1. Doctors shouldn't book more patients than they can see in a day.
2. On December 25, 1968, the *Apollo* 8 astronauts became the first human beings (or people) to see the far side of the moon.
3. Successful lawyers know that they have to work long hours.
4. A person's best friend is a dog. (pronoun removed)
5. My assistant will get you a cup of coffee.
6. Everyone hopes to win the contest. (pronoun removed)
7. The company has assistants to answer the phones.
8. No one believes that superstition!
9. People establish their own "comfort zone" by seeing what they can accomplish in a specific setting.
10. Ask the flight attendant for a cup of tea, please.

Levels of Words

There are only a few times in history when the "F" word has been considered acceptable for use. Here are five of them:

1. "You want WHAT painted on the #$@&% ceiling?" Michelangelo, 1566
2. "Scattered #$@&% showers, my ass." Noah, 4314 B.C.
3. "Where the #$@&% are we?" Amelia Earhart, 1937
4. "Aw, c'mon, Who the #$@&% is going to find out?" Bill Clinton, 1998
5. "Geez, I didn't think they'd get this #$@&% mad." Saddam Hussein, 2003

In Chapter 1, you learned about *usage*, the way people actually use a language. You learned that people adapt their level of usage to their audience and purpose. You know that the "F" word—and other words like it—are not acceptable in business settings and polite company, despite what we see in modern movies and on TV shows.

You always want to suit your words to your readers and listeners. To do so, you have to understand the different levels of diction. Here they are, from most to least formal:

Most formal: Elevated diction
Less formal: Standard American English
Colloquial language
Slang and vernacular
Least formal: Nonstandard English

Let's look at each level of language in detail.

Come Again

Diction is the fancy name for your choice of words. Diction can be described in different ways, such as "formal" and "informal."

1. **Elevated diction**—This type of writing and speech is marked by formal and abstract words, long and complex sentences, a serious tone, and few contractions. It is most commonplace in legal documents, technical reports, the Bible, and other very formal documents.
2. **Standard American English**—This level of speech and writing is distinguished by strict adherence to the rules of grammar and usage that you have learned in this book. It is used in offices, on respected television news shows, and in the magazines and newspapers that educated people (like you) read.
3. **Colloquial language**—This is the speech and writing that you use in casual discourse, such as e-mails, water cooler gossip, and dinner table talks with your near and dear.
4. **Slang and vernacular**—*Slang* is informal vocabulary made of invented words, arbitrarily changed words, or extravagant figures of speech. For example, the term *black eye* or *shiner* is slang for what a doctor would call a "bilateral probital hematoma."

   A word can be both Standard American English or slang, depending on how it is used. The word *say*, for instance, is slang when used at the beginning of a sentence as in "tell me." For example, the following use of the word *say* is considered slang: "Say, how much does that cost?"

Vernacular is comprised of the ordinary language found in a specific region, such as *grinder, hoagie, po' boy,* or *hero* for an overstuffed sandwich.

Be especially careful when you use slang and vernacular language, because it doesn't translate well to different groups and places.

5. **Nonstandard English**—These are the words and phrases you don't ever want to use, as explained in Chapter 1. Examples include the nonstandard "irregardless" for the standard "regardless" and the nonstandard "being that" for the standard "since."

Jargon

A subset of slang is *jargon,* words used in specific professions. All professions have their set of jargon, from a doctor's *stat* for "immediately" to a teacher's use of the term *assessment* for "testing." Sometimes jargon becomes part of Standard American English, such as NASA's terms *lift off, all systems go,* and *countdown.* The following letter is a common Internet joke that uses computer jargon:

> Dear Tech Support:
> Last year I upgraded from Boyfriend 5.0 to Husband 1.0 and noticed a distinct slowdown in overall system performance—particularly in the flower and jewelry applications, which operated flawlessly under Boyfriend 5.0. In addition, Husband 1.0 uninstalled many other valuable programs, such as Romance 9.5 and Personal Attention 6.5, and then installed undesirable programs such as NFL 5.0, NBA 3.0, and Golf Clubs 4.1.

Conversation 8.0 no longer runs, and Housecleaning 2.6 simply crashes the system. I've tried running Nagging 5.3 to fix these problems, but to no avail. What can I do?

Signed,
Desperate

Dear Desperate:
First keep in mind, Boyfriend 5.0 is an Entertainment Package, while Husband 1.0 is an Operating System. Please enter the command: "http: I Thought You Loved Me.htm" and try to download Tears 6.2 and don't forget to install the Guilt 3.0 update. If that application works as designed, Husband 1.0 should then automatically run the applications Jewelry 2.0 and Flowers 3.5. But remember, overuse of the above application can cause Husband 1.0 to default to Grumpy Silence 2.5, Happy Hour 7.0, or Beer 6.1. Beer 6.1 is a very bad program that will download the Snoring Loudly Beta.

Whatever you do, DO NOT install Mother-in-law 1.0 (it runs a virus that will eventually seize control of all your system resources). Also, do not attempt to reinstall the Boyfriend 5.0 program. These are unsupported applications and will crash Husband 1.0. In summary, Husband 1.0 is a great program, but it does have limited memory and cannot learn new applications quickly.

You might consider buying additional software to improve memory and performance. We recommend Hot Food 3.0 and Lingerie 7.7.

Good luck,
Tech Support

As you write and speak, always consider your audience when you decide which level of diction to use. For example, if you are applying for a job in a technical field, you would most likely use jargon in your cover letter and resume to indicate the specific skills you have learned. Using elevated diction in a nightclub would get you branded as a snob, but no one wants a Last Will and Testament written by a lawyer who addresses you as "dude."

Chapter 12

SEX *and the Single Sentence*

Trick question: Which of the following statements is a sentence?

Exhibit A: Think!
Exhibit B: She thinks.
Exhibit C: I know what you're thinking, and you should be ashamed of yourself.

Answer: They are *all* sentences. Once you master the sentence, the basic unit of written communication, you're well on your way to learning how to write with fluency and style. So let's get to it.

Sentence Decoded

So, what *is* a sentence?

As we said, each of the three word groups at the beginning of this chapter is a sentence. That's because they each meet the three requirements for a sentence. To be a sentence, a group of words must . . .

1. have a *subject* (noun or pronoun)
2. have a *predicate* (verb or verb phrase)
3. express a complete thought

Every sentence has two parts: a *subject* and a *predicate.* The subject includes the noun or pronoun that tells what the subject is about. The predicate includes the verb that describes what the subject is doing. Here are some examples of complete sentences:

Complete Sentences with Subjects and Predicates

Subject	Predicate
She	has a wash and wear bridal gown.
I	want a meaningful overnight relationship.
The gene pool	could use a little chlorine.

So, how can *Think!* be a sentence? After all, it's only one word. A command (which is what we have with *Think!*) is considered a sentence because the subject—*you*—is understood. We know that the sentence is really *You think*! Here are a few more examples of commands that function as sentences even though they have only one word:

Stop! **Halt!** **Eat.**

Sentences can be classified in several different ways. One of the most useful ways is by their structure, by the number of independent and dependent clauses they have. Remember that an *independent* clause is a complete sentence, but a *dependent* clause is not. An independent clause, like an independent person, can stand alone. A dependent clause, like a dependent person, cannot stand alone: It must be connected to another sentence. Otherwise, it does not communicate its meaning clearly.

Come Again

An *independent clause* is also called a "sentence." A *dependent clause* is also called a "fragment" or a "sentence fragment" because it is part of a sentence.

The four types of sentences are classified as follows: *simple*, *compound*, *complex*, *compound-complex*. Let's look at each type of sentence in detail.

Simple Sentences

A *simple sentence* has one independent clause. That means it has one subject and one verb, although either or both can be compound. In addition, a simple sentence can have adjectives and adverbs. What a simple sentence can't have is another independent clause or any subordinate clauses. For example:

The $2 bill | turned out to be a fizzle.
subject | predicate | = 1 independent clause

It | was greeted with a lot of media attention.
subject | predicate | = 1 independent clause

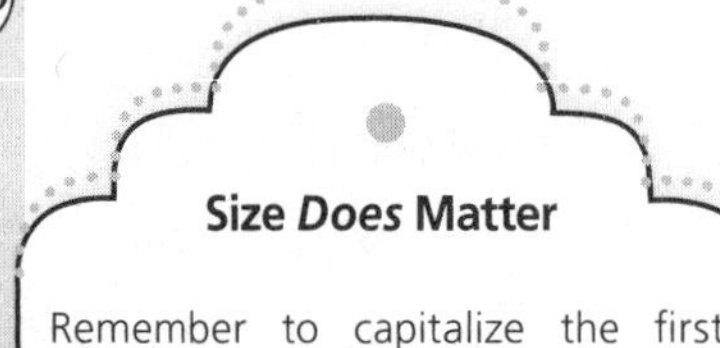

Size *Does* Matter

Remember to capitalize the first word in the complete sentence that comes after a colon.

Compound Sentences

A *compound sentence* is made of two or more independent clauses. The independent clauses can be joined in three different ways: with a coordinating conjunction (*for, and, nor, but, or, yet, so*), with a semicolon (;), or with a colon (:) if the second sentence defines the first. For example:

It is as bad as you think,	and	they are out to get you.
independent clause	coordinating conjunction	independent clause

I'm out of bed and dressed	;	what more do you want?
independent clause	semicolon	independent clause

We have a fixed policy	:	We will not be undersold.
independent clause	colon	independent clause

You may also add a conjunctive adverb to this construction, as in the following example:

I'm out of bed and dressed	;	after all,	what more do you want?
independent clause	semicolon	conjunctive adverb	independent clause

To refresh your memory, here are some conjunctive adverbs: *however, nevertheless, nonetheless, as a result, notwithstanding.*

Complex Sentences

A *complex sentence* contains one independent clause and at least one dependent clause. The independent clause is called the "main clause." These sentences use *subordinating conjunctions* to link ideas. For example:

Ice cream will actually make you feel warmer rather than cooler (independent clause) because (subordinating conjunction) it contains so many calories (dependent clause).

Although (subordinating conjunction) people believe that skyscrapers can sway eight feet or more in a strong wind (dependent clause), this is really not true (independent clause).

To refresh your memory, here are some subordinating conjunctions: *after, although, as, because, before, if, since, though, unless, until, when, whenever, where, wherever, while.*

Show and Tell

If the dependent clause comes first in the sentence, it is set off with a comma.

Compound-Complex Sentences

A *compound-complex sentence* has at least two independent clauses and at least one dependent clause. The dependent clause can be part of the independent clause. For example:

A person who weighs 120 pounds can lose 13 pounds a year without dieting
independent clause

if he or she goes for a walk four times a week and
subordinating conjunction / dependent clause / coordinating conjunction

covers 3 miles in an hour each time.
independent clause

"Every American bride is taken to Niagara Falls, and
independent clause / coordinating conjunction

the sight must be one of the keenest disappointments in American married life
independent clause

if not the keenest one." (Oscar Wilde)
subordinating conjunction / dependent clause

One type of sentence is not better than the other. Simple sentences are no less worthy than complex ones. Rather, each type of sentence has its own specific use. For a general audience, a mix of sentences is best because it makes your writing varied and interesting.

Drive It On Home

Label each sentence type in the following anecdotes:

(1) Once G. K. Chesterton and several other famous writers were asked what one book they would take with them if they were stranded on a desert island. (2) "I would take *The Complete Works of William Shakespeare*," answered one writer, but another said, "I'd choose the Bible instead." (3) Chesterton was asked what book he would select. (4) "I would choose *Thomas's Guide to Practical Shipbuilding*," he replied.

(5) Brendan Behan, late Irish author, was the soul of courtesy, but there were times when he had to respond. (6) Behan and a friend were emerging from the Long Hall in Dublin during the Christmas season, and Behan had the misfortune to bump into a lady laden with parcels, thus scattering her parcels all over the pavement. (7) Brendan promptly stooped to recover them from among the feet of the passersby and restore them to her arms, but her ladyship's temper was not satisfied. (8) "I'd have you know," she declared angrily, "that my husband's a detective; if he was here, he'd take ye!" (9) Brendan replied, "Ma'am, I don't doubt it for a second. (10) If he took you, he'd take anything."

Answers:

1. complex
2. compound
3. simple
4. simple
5. compound
6. compound-complex
7. compound
8. compound-complex
9. simple
10. complex

Drive It On Home

The following passages are comprised of simple sentences only. It's soooo boring. Combine the sentences to make the writing zing. Keep some simple sentences if you wish, but combine other sentences to make compound, complex, and compound-complex sentences as well.

1. The famous writer Somerset Maugham was in London. He was recovering from the flu. His phone rang. It was a female admirer. She asked, "Can I send you fruit? Would you rather have flowers?" The eighty-eight-year-old Maugham responded: "Too late for fruit. Too early for flowers."

   ____

   ____

   ____

   ____

   ____

2. Playwright George S. Kaufman attended the opening night of a show. He was asked for his opinion. He said, "It is not fair for me to say. I saw the play under especially unfortunate circumstances. The curtain was up."

   ____

   ____

   ____

   ____

   ____

3. Hank Aaron was up to bat for the first time in his major-league career. The catcher for the opposing team tried to rattle him. The catcher said, “Hey, kid, you’re holding your bat all wrong. You should hold it with the label up. Then you could read it.” Aaron replied, “I didn’t come here to read.”

____

____

____

____

____

Sample Answers:

1. The famous writer Somerset Maugham was in London, recovering from the flu. His phone rang, and a female admirer asked, “Can I send you fruit or would you rather have flowers?” The eighty-eight-year-old Maugham responded: “Too late for fruit—too early for flowers.”
2. After he had attended the opening night of a show, playwright George S. Kaufman was asked for his opinion. He said, “It is not fair for me to say because I saw the play under especially unfortunate circumstances: The curtain was up.”
3. When Hank Aaron was up to bat for the first time in his major-league career, the catcher for the opposing team tried to rattle him by saying, “Hey, kid, you’re holding your bat all wrong. You should hold it with the label up so you could read it.” Aaron replied, “I didn’t come here to read.”

Writing Complete Sentences

Logically, sentences have to be complete to communicate their meaning. Well, yes and no.

- *Yes*, sentences must be complete when you're writing any business and professional communication. That's because your audience expects completeness and clarity in your written communication.
- *No*, sentences don't have to be complete when you're writing dialogue or interior monologues in a short story, novel, or play. That's because your audience expects your writing in these genres to capture the way that people really talk.

But before you can start playing around with your sentences, let's make sure we're all on the same page when it comes to making them correct and complete.

Run-ons

A *run-on sentence* is two incorrectly joined independent clauses. The error is called a *comma splice* if a comma is inserted where the two independent clauses run together. When independent clauses are run together, readers can't follow the ideas. Here are two examples:

The vegetables were fresh they were tasty.

The first diamonds were discovered along riverbeds in South Central India, they were found around 800 b.c.

There are several different ways to correct a run-on. First, you can separate the run-on into two sentences with end punctuation such as periods, exclamation marks, and question marks. Or, you can add a coordinating conjunction (*and, nor, but, or, for, yet, so*) or a semicolon to create a compound sentence. Third, add a subordinating conjunction to create a complex sentence. Last, rewrite the sentence to correct the error. Here are some examples:

The vegetables were fresh. They were tasty.
(two separate sentences)

The vegetables were fresh, and they were tasty.
(compound sentence with independent clauses joined by a coordinating conjunction)

The vegetables were fresh; they were tasty.
(compound sentence with independent clauses joined by a semicolon)

Since the vegetables were fresh, they were tasty.
(complex sentence)

The fresh vegetables were great.
(sentence rewritten to eliminate the error)

Drive It On Home

Correct the run-on as directed in each sentence.

1. The first diamonds were discovered along riverbeds in South Central India, they were found around 800 B.C.
   Rewrite as two separate sentences:
   ____
   ____

2. The first diamonds were discovered along riverbeds in South Central India, they were found around 800 B.C.
   Rewrite as a compound sentence with independent clauses joined by a coordinating conjunction:
   ____
   ____

3. The first diamonds were discovered along riverbeds in South Central India, they were found around 800 B.C.
   Rewrite as a compound sentence with independent clauses joined by a semicolon:
   ____
   ____

4. The first diamonds were discovered along riverbeds in South Central India, they were found around 800 B.C.

Rewrite as a complex sentence:

____

____

5. The first diamonds were discovered along riverbeds in South Central India, they were found around 800 B.C.
   Rewrite sentence to eliminate the error:

   ____

   ____

Sample Answers:

1. The first diamonds were discovered along riverbeds in South Central India. They were found around 800 B.C.
2. The first diamonds were discovered along riverbeds in South Central India, and they were found around 800 B.C.
3. The first diamonds were discovered along riverbeds in South Central India; they were found around 800 B.C.
4. The first diamonds were discovered along riverbeds in South Central India, when they were found around 800 B.C.
5. The first diamonds were discovered along riverbeds in South Central India around 800 B.C.

Which revision do you choose to use in your own writing? Choose the one that best suits your audience and purpose. As you choose, consider which version is most clear and well stated.

Sentence Interruptus: Fragments

As its name suggests, a *sentence fragment* is a group of words that do not express a complete thought. Most times, a fragment is missing a subject, a verb, or both. Other times, a fragment may have a subject and a verb but still not express a complete thought. Fragments can be very long as well as very short, so don't be fooled by length. Here are some examples:

Because New Jersey has the most people per square mile.
Parents who allow their children to have pets.
Simply by watching fish in an aquarium.
When a pet owner gets home late at night after a hard day's work.
Since Kahlil Gibran, author of *The Prophet* and many other works, died in 1931 at age forty-eight.

You can correct a fragment by adding the missing part to the sentence or deleting the word that creates the fragment. These are often subordinating conjunctions or relative pronouns (*who, whom, which*, etc.). You can also rewrite the sentence, of course. You can *always* rewrite a sentence, which is what gives English its wonderful flexibility. Here are some examples.

Because New Jersey has the most people per square mile, housing is in short supply.
(missing part added)

~~Because~~ New Jersey has the most people per square mile.
(subordinating conjunction deleted)

Drive It On Home

Correct the fragments as directed in each sentence.

1. Parents who allow their children to have pets
   (add the missing part):

   ____

2. Parents who allow their children to have pets
   (delete the relative pronoun)

3. Simply by watching fish in an aquarium
   (add the missing part):

   ____

4. Simply by watching fish in an aquarium
   (rewrite the sentence):

   ____

5. When a pet owner gets home late at night after a hard day's work.
   (delete the subordinating conjunction)

6. When a pet owner gets home late at night after a hard days' work.
   (add the missing part):

   ____

7. Since Kahlil Gibran, author of *The Prophet* and many other works, died in 1931 at age forty-eight.
   (delete the subordinating conjunction)

8. Since Kahlil Gibran, author of *The Prophet* and many other works, died in 1931 at age forty-eight.
   (add the missing part):

   ____

   ____

Sample Answers:

1. Parents who allow their children to have pets often have better-adjusted children.
2. Parents allow their children to have pets.
3. Simply by watching fish in an aquarium, people can reduce their level of stress.
4. Watch the fish in an aquarium!
5. A pet owner gets home late at night after a hard day's work.
6. When a pet owner gets home late at night after a hard day's work, the pet will need immediate attention.
7. Kahlil Gibran, author of *The Prophet* and many other works, died in 1931 at age forty-eight.
8. Since Kahlil Gibran, author of *The Prophet* and many other works, died in 1931 at age forty-eight, all his royalties have been paid to the people in his home village in Lebanon.

Smarty Pants

In her short story "Imagined Scenes," Ann Beattie uses fragments to capture the way the characters really talk. Here's an excerpt:

"Pretty," David says.

"Where would that be?"

"Greece?"

Drive It On Home

Correct the run-ons and fragments in these sentences.

1. Sports should be fun, some people make them onerous.
2. Tornadoes can be perilous storms they can pick up a house and drop it hundreds of feet away.
3. While most shark meat is processed for consumption.
4. Although many sharks are caught by fishermen for sport. Sharks can and do sustain small businesses.
5. Their skins providing a hide tougher than leather, out of which boots are fabricated.

Correct the run-ons and fragments in this passage.

6. Ten men and one woman hanging onto a rope beneath a hovering helicopter. Fearing the rope was not strong enough to carry them all. They decided one must drop off or all would fall, the woman graciously said that she would let go of the rope. Because as a woman. She was used to giving up everything for her husband and children. Without getting anything in return. When she finished her speech. All the men clapped.

Sample Answers:

1. Sports should be fun, but some people make them onerous.
2. Tornadoes can be perilous storms; they can pick up a house and drop it hundreds of feet away.
3. Most shark meat is processed for consumption.
4. Although many sharks are caught by fishermen for sport, sharks can and do sustain small businesses.
5. Their skins provide a hide tougher than leather, out of which boots are fabricated.
6. Ten men and one woman were hanging onto a rope beneath a hovering helicopter. Fearing the rope was not strong enough to carry them all, they decided one must drop off or all would fall. The woman graciously said that she would let go of the rope because as a woman, she was used to giving up everything for her husband and children without getting anything in return. When she finished her speech, all the men clapped.

Active and Passive Voice

As you consider the structure of your sentences, you decide whether to have the subject perform the action or receive the action. Here are two examples:

Laura found my bracelet.
(subject performs action)

My bracelet was found by Laura.
(subject receives action)

This is called *voice*. English has two voices: active and passive. In the *active voice*, the subject performs the action. In the *passive voice*, the subject receives the action. For instance:

Active Voice:
My dog ate the toothpaste.
He had minty-fresh breath.
We bought fresh toothpaste.

Passive Voice:
The toothpaste was eaten by my dog.
Minty-fresh breath was had by him.
Fresh toothpaste was bought. (Notice that the subject is not named here.)

As a general rule, use the active voice instead of the passive voice. The active voice is more direct and concise, which makes it clearer. You want to be direct and concise in writing unless you work at a university, Congress, or the post office. In these cases, it's better to make all speech and writing as wordy and difficult to understand as possible.

There are two instances where the passive voice is preferable over the active voice. Here they are:

1. Use the passive voice when you don't want to assign blame to or emphasize who or what performed the action. This is especially important in business if you ever want to get promoted. Here's an example:
   A mistake was made.
   The windows were left open during the weekend.

2. Use the passive voice when you don't know who did the action.
   The package was shipped at 10:02 A.M.
   All the cookies were eaten.

Drive It On Home

Label each of the following sentences *active* or *passive.* Then rewrite the passive sentences in the active voice.

1. Man says to God, "God, why were women made so beautiful by you?"
2. God says, "So you would love them."
3. "But God," the man says, "why was she made so dumb by you?"
4. God says, "So she would love you."
5. A teacher was told by a pupil that a cat was found by him.
6. The cat was dead.
7. "How did you know the cat was dead?" the child was asked by the teacher.
8. "Because I pissed in its ear and it didn't move," answered the child.
9. "What was done by you?" the teacher exclaimed.
10. "You know," the boy said, "I leaned over and went *'Pssst!'* and it didn't move."

Answers:

1. Passive
   Rewritten: Man says to God, "God, why did you make women so beautiful?"
2. Active

3. Passive

   Rewritten: "But God," the man says, "why did you make them so dumb?"

4. Active
5. Passive

   Rewritten: A pupil told his teacher that he found a cat.

6. Active
7. Passive

   Rewritten: "How did you know the cat was dead?" the teacher asked.

8. Active
9. Passive

   Rewritten: "What did you do?" the teacher exclaimed.

10. Active

Chapter 13
Work It, Baby: *Let's Get Some* STYLE

A novice writer once asked Dr. Samuel Johnson (1709–1784), the creator of the first modern dictionary, for his opinion of a piece that the young man had written. "Sir," Johnson supposedly responded, "this piece is both original and good. Unfortunately, the parts that are original are not good, and the parts that are good are not original."

In this chapter, you'll learn how to make your writing both original *and* good.

Can Those Clichés

How many of these phrases have you heard or read recently?

- real time
- need to know
- state of the art
- next generation
- cutting edge
- bottom line

If you think you've heard these phrases a lot, you're right—and you're not suffering the effects of Happy Hour. These phrases *are* bandied about 24/7, with wild abandon, big time, and famously. They send a message all right. What's the message? Writing filled with *clichés*—stale descriptive expressions—is flabby and lazy. As a result, it's not worth the effort of reading.

Clichés weaken your writing because they're boring. They signal your reader to zone off because the text is so predictable. They're trite, hackneyed, and ho-hum. The famous language pundit George Orwell (author of *Animal Farm* and *1984*) described clichés as the huge dump of worn-out metaphors that have lost all evocative power. They are used because they save people the trouble of inventing phrases for themselves. Further, clichés date your writing because they are very temporal: Here today, gone tomorrow, as the cliché goes.

Replace clichés with fresh new language. Go for exciting comparisons, vivid words and phrases, and sensory images.

Drive It On Home

At one time, every cliché was as fresh as a daisy, really top-notch, outside the box. Now, alas, they are as stale as yesterday's news. Let's see if we can give these clichés a wake-up call at this point in time. To do so, first define each cliché. Then rewrite it to make it communicate clearly and vigorously. But don't get all hot and bothered, dude.

1. going postal ______________________
2. eye candy ______________________
3. the bridge-and-tunnel crowd ______________________
4. the Greatest Generation ______________________
5. that is so over; stick a fork in it ______________________
6. my bad ______________________
7. you go, girlfriend ______________________
8. don't even go there ______________________
9. cut to the chase ______________________
10. be proactive ______________________

Sample Answers:

The way that you rewrite the clichés will vary, but all revisions should have specific details and precise language. Go for a clever turn of phrase, too.

1. losing all control and attacking others
2. attractive person, often used as a decoration
3. commuters (derisive term)
4. people in their prime during World War II
5. yesterday's news
6. my mistake
7. a term of encouragement
8. don't discuss the issue
9. get to the point
10. take action

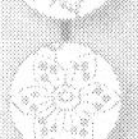

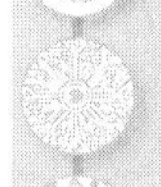

SMARTY PANTS

Between 1935 and 1952, the humorist Frank Sullivan wrote a series of essays for the *New Yorker* in the guise of Mr. Arbuthnot, the cliché expert. In this role, Sullivan testified on the trite expressions and hackneyed phrases of the day. Some of his essays are posted on the Internet. Look for them; they're well worth the read.

Be Original, Not Weird

In their attempt to craft fresh and evocative comparisons, some writers veer from original to downright kinky. It happens more often than you think, like tofu jambalaya and other notable nouvelle cuisine failures. Here are a few notable failures in metaphor:

The hailstones leaped from the pavement, just like maggots when you fry them in hot grease.

He fell for her like his heart was a mob informant and she was the East River.

So it hurt, the way your tongue does when you accidentally staple it to the wall.

She grew on him like she was a colony of E. coli and he was room-temperature Canadian beef.

She had a deep, throaty, genuine laugh, like that sound a dog makes before it throws up.

Point made. Be creative, not cranky.

Get to the Point!

A husband was reading the newspaper and came upon a study that said women use more words than men. Excited to prove to his wife that he had been right when he accused her of talking too much, he showed her the study results. It read, "Men use about 15,000 words per day, but women use 30,000."

The wife thought for a while, then she said to her husband, "It's because we have to repeat everything we say."

The husband said, "What?"

Some writers feel an obligation to say everything twice. Or three times. Or four times. Perhaps they feel the audience isn't paying attention; perhaps they don't recognize the redundancy. They repeat words, phrases, and even entire sentences in a different guise. Trust me—people *are* listening. And if they're not, it's their problem, not yours.

Be Concise

From now on, omit unnecessary words or ideas that you have already stated. Use a lot of important detail, but no unnecessary words. You want your writing to be *concise*, direct, and to the point. Wordy writing annoys your readers because it forces them to hack their way through your sentences before they can understand what you're saying. Neat, well-organized sentences, like neat, well-organized closets, make life so much easier.

The following chart shows some wordy phrases and their concise revisions. Notice how well they communicate meaning without their excess baggage.

Cut Extra Words

Wordy	Revised
covered over	covered
true facts	facts
sum total; end result	result
most unique	unique
proceed ahead	proceed

Drive It On Home

Rewrite each of the following phrases to eliminate the unnecessary words.

1. new innovation ____________________
2. small in size ____________________
3. extra gratuity ____________________
4. continue to remain ____________________
5. combine together ____________________
6. repeat again ____________________
7. green in color ____________________
8. few in number ____________________
9. complete stop ____________________
10. final end ____________________

Answers:

1. innovation
2. small
3. gratuity
4. remain
5. combine
6. repeat
7. green
8. few
9. stop
10. end

The following chart shows some common windy phrases. Cut the air from their sails as shown.

Cut Wordy Phrases

Wordy	Revised
at this point in time	now
for the purpose of	for
in the event that	if
because of the fact that	because
due to the fact that	because
weather event	rain (etc.)
experience some discomfort	hurt

SMARTY PANTS

Winston Churchill once said, "Old words are best, and short words best of all."

Drive It On Home

Rewrite each of the following sentences to eliminate the unnecessary words.

1. The criminal was completely surrounded on all sides.
2. As I have reiterated over and over again, make your writing concise.
3. The point I am trying to make is that you never really learn to swear until you learn to drive.
4. In a very real sense, as long as there are tests, there will be prayer in public schools.
5. Whatever happened to Preparations A through G? That is what I mean to say.

Answers:

1. The criminal was ~~completely~~ surrounded. ~~on all sides~~.
2. As I have repeated, ~~reiterated over and over again,~~ make your writing concise.
3. ~~The point I am trying to make is that~~ you never really learn to swear until you learn to drive.
4. ~~In a very real sense,~~ as long as there are tests, there will be prayer in public schools.
5. Whatever happened to Preparations A through G? ~~That is what I mean to say.~~

Revise Wordy Paragraphs

Writers often get carried away by the sound of their own words. "Not me!" you yelp. Yes, you, buckaroo, and sometimes even me. That's why editors were invented. Most of the time, however, we're not lucky enough to have an editor, so we have to do the job ourselves. It's not an easy job because each word is near and dear to your heart, like your eight-track tapes and the pants that haven't fit in decades.

You want to save every one of your words; after all, they are *your* words. "Eliminate that sentence?" you howl. "I can't possibly cut such a superb (graceful, important, dazzling) sentence." Yes, you can; trust me. And your writing will be the better for it. An effective writing style is concise.

Feel the pain with me. How could your revise the following paragraph to eliminate wordiness? You can move words, phrases, and sentences as well as remove unnecessary parts.

My grandma and grandpa came to America from Italy. They brought from Italy their heritage. Their heritage is part of my sister and me. My mother passed this heritage down to us. We as a people could never escape or run away from our heritage. It is what makes us what we are today. My grandmother was born in Palermo, Italy, which makes her Sicilian. My grandfather was born in Calabria, which makes him Calabrese. This heritage that I have obtained will always be in my bloodlines. I would never want to escape it.

Here's a variation:

My grandmother was born in Palermo, Italy, so she is Sicilian. My grandfather was born in Calabria, so he is Calabrese. They brought their heritage to America and passed it down to my family. It is what makes us what we are today.

Drive It On Home

Eliminate the wordiness in the following passages.

1. Great love and great achievements involve great risk. I believe this statement to be true. When I look at the world and all the people in the world, I see that everything we accomplish involves some degree of risk, whether it be big or small risk, it is still a risk. Love itself is a big risk. Perhaps the biggest risk of all is love because when you find that special someone you place the rest of your life on the line to be with that someone.
2. It is obvious in today's society that both men and women are involved in athletics. However, the women are treated very differently than the

men are treated. What does Title IX exactly mean? Title IX of the Education Amendment of 1972 is a federal statute that was created to prohibit sex discrimination in education programs that receive financial assistance. The main issue that Title IX deals with is equal opportunities for women in athletics and men, too. Title IX affects both men and women. All groups can be affected negatively, positively, or both. The basis of Title IX is to benefit women who are already in athletics or young girls who are entering the world of athletics. The basis of Title IX is to get equal opportunities for both men's and women's teams. This will give male and female athletes the same chances.

3. I am requesting the use of a community public-address (PA) system. A public-address system is a piece of equipment that amplifies the speaker's voice so that it can be heard at a distance. The reason that we are making this request for a PA system is because we are planning to set up a stage to address the audience and a booth on the side to sell merchandise at the Annual Community Fair.

Sample Answers:

1. Great love and great achievements involve great risk. Perhaps the biggest risk of all is love because it involves commitment and sacrifice.
2. Today, both men and women are involved in athletics. Title IX of the Education Amendment of 1972 is a federal statute created to prohibit sex discrimination in education programs that receive financial assistance.
3. We request the use of a community public-address (PA) system for the Annual Community Fair.

The Devil's in the Details

Adding details to your writing spices it up and makes it that much more interesting, as well as clear. Choose details that help you write clearly and directly. You want readers to understand your message, visualize your topic, and take the action that you may require.

How can you recognize details in sentences or paragraphs? Details will fall into these six main categories:

1. *Examples* illustrate your point. Use examples to help a reader understand a general statement by giving specific information that represents one piece of the whole concept.
2. *Facts* are statements that can be proven. For example, the statement "Mount Rainier Park was established by Congress in 1899" is a fact. It can be verified, and there are no reasonable arguments against it.
3. *Statistics* are numbers used to give additional information. Statistics can be presented in different ways, such as charts, graphs, lists, percentages, and decimals.
4. *Reasons* tell *why* something happened.
5. *Definitions* explain what something means. Definitions often come from the dictionary.
6. *Descriptions* are words or phrases that tell how something looks, smells, tastes, sounds, or feels. Descriptions use sensory words to help readers visualize or get a mental picture of what they are reading.

Sometimes a detail can be neatly assigned to one of these categories. Often, however, the details can be classified in different ways. An example will often include a description and a statistic. So don't sweat the classification; just make sure that you include a lot of juicy details!

As you read the following paragraph, see which details you find especially effective. Which ones appeal to the five senses?

> In 1869, Antonio López de Santa Anna, the Mexican leader of the Alamo attack, went into exile on Staten Island, New York. Santa Anna had brought with him several objects from home, including a large lump of chicle, the elastic sap of the sapodilla tree. The Mayan Indians had been chewing this substance for hundreds of years. Santa Anna wasn't interested in chewing the chicle; instead, he hoped that the inventor Thomas Adams could refine the substance into a substitute for rubber. Adams did his best, but he couldn't transform chicle into rubber.
>
> One day, Santa Anna had an inspiration: Why not use the chicle as the Mayans did? He immersed the chicle in water until it was soft and pressed it into little round shapes. They were a drab gray, but every single ball of "gum" sold the very next day. With his profits, Adams went into business producing Adams New York Gum No. 1.
>
> The process of making chewing gum is surprisingly similar today. Now, small pieces of latex—still obtained from the sapodilla trees of Central and South America—are kneaded until soft. Today, however, the chicle is added to a hot sugar–corn syrup mixture. When the mixture is smooth, it is flavored, usually with mint, and rolled into thin strips or squares.

Drive It On Home

As you read the following paragraph, notice how the writer uses vivid details. Then place the details into categories on the lines that follow. You can place a detail in more than one category, since classifications often overlap.

This is the story of how a rugged American symbol was born by a sudden inspiration. In 1850, twenty-one-year-old Levi Strauss traveled from New York to San Francisco. A peddler, Strauss took needles, thread, pots, pans, ribbons, yarn, scissors, buttons, and canvas across the country to sell to the gold miners. The small items sold well, but Strauss found himself stuck with the rolls of canvas because it was not heavy enough to be used for tents. While talking to one of the miners, Strauss learned that sturdy pants that would stand up to the rigors of digging were almost impossible to find. On the spot, Strauss measured the man with a piece of string. For $6 in gold dust, Strauss had a piece of the leftover canvas made into a pair of stiff, rugged pants. The miner was delighted with the results, and word got around about "those pants of Levi's." Business was so good that Levi Strauss was soon out of canvas. He wrote to his two brothers in New York to send more. He received instead a tough brown cotton cloth made in Nîmes, France, called *serge de Nîmes*. Almost at once, the foreign term was shortened to *denim*. Strauss had the cloth dyed a rich blue called "indigo," which became a company trademark. These were the humble beginnings of a fashion that would take the world by storm.

Examples:

____

____

Facts:

____

____

Statistics:

____

____

Reasons:

____

____

Definitions:

____

____

Descriptions:

____

____

SAMPLE ANSWERS:

Examples: A peddler, Strauss took needles, thread, pots, pans, ribbons, yarn, scissors, buttons, and canvas across the country to sell to the gold miners

Facts: Twenty-one-year-old Levi Strauss traveled from New York to San Francisco; The small items sold well; which became a company trademark

Statistics: In 1850; For $6 in gold dust

Reasons: A peddler; to sell to the gold miners; Strauss found himself stuck with the rolls of canvas because it was not heavy enough to be used for tents; While talking to one of the miners, Strauss learned that sturdy pants that would stand up to the rigors of digging were almost impossible to find; Business was so good that Levi Strauss was soon out of canvas

Definitions: a tough brown cotton cloth made in Nîmes, France, called *serge de Nîmes;* Almost at once, the foreign term was shortened to *denim*; rich blue called "indigo"

Descriptions: rugged American symbol; sudden inspiration; needles, thread, pots, pans, ribbons, yarn, scissors, buttons, and canvas; Strauss measured the man with a piece of string; stiff, rugged pants; "those pants of Levi's"; a tough brown cotton cloth made in Nîmes, France, called *serge de Nîmes*; rich blue called "indigo"

Drive It On Home

Add some vivid words to the following paragraph. Feel free to do some research, if you wish.

In Japan, ______________ relish aquatic fly larvae sautéed in sugar and ______________ . Venezuelans feast on ______________ fire-roasted tarantulas. Many South Africans adore ______________ termites with ______________ porridge. Merchants in Cambodia sell cooked cicadas by the ______________. Diners cut off the ______________ and ______________ before eating them. People in Bali remove the ______________ from dragonflies and boil the bodies in ______________ milk and ______________.

Sample Answers:

In Japan, gourmets relish aquatic fly larvae sautéed in sugar and soy sauce. Venezuelans feast on fresh fire-roasted tarantulas. Many South Africans adore fried termites with cornmeal porridge. Merchants in Cambodia sell cooked cicadas by the bagful. Diners cut off the wings and legs before eating them. People in Bali remove the wings from dragonflies and boil the bodies in coconut milk and garlic.

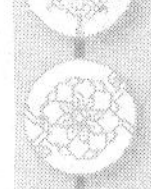
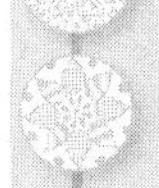

Chapter 14

WRITE *This Way*

If you spend much time working on a computer, someone may have already forwarded you a list like the following one:

You know you are living in the twenty-first century when . . .

1. You accidentally enter your password on the microwave.
2. You haven't played solitaire with real cards in years.
3. You don't stay in touch with friends because they don't have e-mail.
4. You've sat at the same desk for four years and worked for three different companies.
5. Contractors outnumber permanent staff and are more likely to get long-service awards.
6. You learn about your company going out of business on the eleven o'clock news.

7. As you read this list, you think about forwarding it to your "friends."
8. You got this e-mail from a friend who never talks to you anymore, except to send you jokes from the Web.

No doubt about it: Written communication has changed. Gone are the days of long, leisurely letters sent via snail mail. Today, electronic communication is fast becoming the writing form and forum of choice. Novels are being published on the Web; people meet and greet, mate and break up in cyberspace. To stay in the race, you have to know how to write effective e-mails. Of course, there's still a big place for business and personal letters, so we'll cover all three forms of writing in this chapter.

E-mail

E-mail is an abbreviation for *electronic mail,* the transmission of messages over an electronic communications network. E-mail works like the post office—only a lot faster!—to transmit messages over computer networks to individuals and groups. To send an e-mail, you need two things: a computer that's linked to the Internet and the person's e-mail address. Here's how they work:

Be Afraid, Be Very Afraid

E-mail seems so delightfully informal, like going to the supermarket in sweatpants and flip-flops. Don't be tricked by the seeming casualness of e-mail: It's still a written document. Whether you're handing your letter to Pete the postal carrier or whizzing it through cyberspace via e-mail, the effect is the same: You're putting your words down in writing for someone else

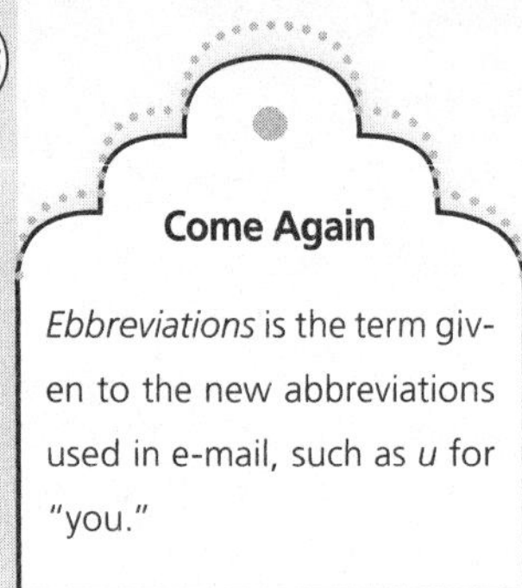

Come Again

Ebbreviations is the term given to the new abbreviations used in e-mail, such as *u* for "you."

to read, destroy, or share with others. Too many people have been spotted in the supermarket looking like unmade beds; too many people have written sloppy or scurrilous e-mails. The former is laughable; the latter, downright dangerous to your career.

Thus, write all e-mail as you would any important written communication. Follow these steps as you write e-mail:

1. *Compose your document offline.* You can write your e-mail directly online or you can draft it offline and upload it later. If the document has the slightest chance of being important, resist the temptation to toss off a speedy reply. Instead, draft the letter in your word-processing program so you can let it sit before you send it. Once you push that "send" button, you've lost the chance to rethink your words. Remember, e-mail sent and received in an office can be used in legal proceedings.
2. *Stay professional.* English teachers the world over initially rejoiced when we heard about e-mail, especially IMs (instant messages). "So many chances for people to practice writing," we chortled in glee. "Oh, how the writing will improve," we beamed. Alas, it was not to be. If anything, e-mail and IMs have caused the greatest destruction to communication since the invention of the telephone.

   For some odd reason, people feel that when it comes to e-mail, they can disregard the accepted conventions of grammar, usage, spelling, and punctuation. To make the matter even more lamentable, people use lazy, bastardized abbreviations such as *4* for "for," *b4* for "before," and *u* for "you." This slop is getting carried over into other forms of writing as well. Isn't it bad enough that on airplanes we have to sit next to codgers in Speedoes? Now we have to deal with "ebbreviations" in formal documents.

How can we stop this rising tide of miscommunication? You're the beachhead, cupcake.

As with any written communication, e-mail can become a legal document. Therefore, before you send your message, review it carefully to make sure it conveys your precise meaning and is free of errors in grammar, spelling, punctuation, and usage. And don't use any of those dopey ebbreviations.

Size *Does* Matter

Many of my students have, um, *amusing* e-mail addresses, like BigWeenie, HotStuff69, and SweetCheeks. These may be appropriate scribbled on a napkin in a club at 2:00 A.M., but they're tacky in the world of work. Make sure your screen name is professional. If it's not, odds are that your recipient is going to think you're selling penile enhancements and delete your e-mail without ever reading it.

3. *Include a subject line.* The *subject line* is a brief description of the message. An effective subject line grabs your reader's attention and summarizes the content of the e-mail. As an added courtesy, if your message doesn't require a reply, type FYI (for your information) at the beginning of the subject line. This is especially important if your screen name is not similar to your real name or is sexually piggy in some way—like HotBuns69.

4. *Be brief.* Write concise messages and make your point fast. In general, make your sentences and paragraphs shorter than you would in a letter, memo, or other offline communication. Further, place the most important facts first. These might include results or recommendations, for example. Busy readers will appreciate your consideration—and you'll get better results.
5. *Sign your name.* Always sign your name on the bottom of your e-mail or put it in the header. This way, the recipient won't be trying to figure out who you are and why you sent this e-mail.

Drive It On Home

Correct the following e-mail.

```
Subj:
Date:  12/10/04
From:  CuteTPie@aol.com
To:    Laurie_Rozakis@Farmingdale.edu
```

Sent from the Internet (Details)

```
Hey Doc,
Can u meet me b4 class on Monday b/c I missed class
last week. i need the work :-).
Thanx
```

Sample Answer:

```
Subj: Making up the work that I missed December 6-8
Date: 12/10/04
From: Alyssa Peterson (CuteTPie@aol.com)
To:   Laurie_Rozakis@Farmingdale.edu
```

Sent from the Internet (Details)

```
Dr. Rozakis,
   Would you be able to meet me in your office before class
on Monday, December 13? I missed class last week and I
would like to discuss making up the work that I missed.
   Thank you for your consideration in this matter.
   Alyssa
```

Mind Your Own Business

Business letters haven't been replaced by e-mail, even if many of them are sent that way. Successful business writers know that an effective business letter must fulfill very specific requirements. These include:

- Meeting the reader's needs
- Arranging all information clearly
- Cementing the relationship between writer and reader
- Building goodwill
- Giving a good impression of the writer's company or organization

- Eliminating or reducing the need to communicate further on the same issue
- Doing business ethically and fairly
- Using an appropriate business tone
- Handling difficult situations with grace and professionalism
- Following a set format

Come Again

A *template* is a premade pattern. Your word-processing program has different styles of templates for business letters, memos, resumes, and more. Try them all to see which variations you like the best.

All business letters follow a standard format. They are always typed on 8½" × 11" paper, single-spaced, one side only. Word-processing programs include templates for business letters, which makes formatting a snap.

Here are the three standard formats for business letters. The differences among the three styles relate to paragraph indentations and the placement of headings and closings.

- *The block style*: all parts of the letter are placed flush left.
- *The modified block style*: the heading is in the upper right corner; the closing and signature are in the lower right corner, parallel to the heading. The paragraphs are *not* indented.
- *The semiblock style*: the heading is placed in the upper right corner and the close and signature in the lower right corner, parallel to the heading. The paragraphs *are* indented.

All documents are automatically left-justified. This means that the left-hand margin is straight, not ragged. In addition, you can justify the right-hand margin. Right-justification lets you fit about 20 percent more text on the page. However, use right-justification only with proportional fonts (such as Times New Roman) to avoid distracting, wide spaces between words.

Model Business Letter

Following is a sample business letter to use as a model. The text to the left of the letter points out the key features of an effective business letter as they were listed earlier in this chapter.

letter follows a set format

July 20, 2004

Dr. Laurie Rozakis
45 Anywhere Road
Anytown, Anyplace 11771

Dear Dr. Rozakis:

most important information first; tone builds goodwill

It is with great pleasure that we invite you to participate as a reader at Step's twentieth annual Long Island Family Reading Fun Fest at the Rocky Point University Student Center in Rocky Point, New York, to be held Saturday, September 18, from 10:00 A.M. to 4:00 P.M.

meets the reader's needs

This event is cosponsored by the Council for the Promotion of Reading in conjunction with Rocky Point University and a number of Long Island's public libraries, literacy organizations, and educational institutions. The goal of the event is to celebrate reading as a fun, enlightening, and enjoyable activity for the entire family.

cements the relationship between the reader and writer

This day of family literacy will include authors and celebrities reading to children and their families, literacy-based entertainment, hands-on arts and crafts, learning workshops, and more. A book fair will provide opportunities for parents and children to speak with authors and to purchase your books. Complimentary refreshments will be available in our authors' booth.

gives a good impression of the organization and event

Last year the event was a success with more than 3,500 adults and children attending. Because of last year's achievement, we anticipate an even larger audience this year.

meets the reader's needs by providing information

If you are available to participate, please think about the book(s) you would like to read, the approximate age groups you would like to address, and the times you would like to present. We are inviting you to read for approximately 20 to 25 minutes. Times available are 11:00 A.M., 12:00 P.M., 1:00 P.M., 2:00 P.M., and 3:00 P.M. In addition, we offer authors a free exhibit table, giving you an opportunity to sell your book(s).

tone builds goodwill; provides needed information

Thank you for helping us promote literacy to children and families across Long Island. RSVP to Harvey Wattle at 631-555-5561 or Harvey_Wattle@step.org. We look forward to having you share in our celebration of reading and literacy on Long Island.

tone builds goodwill; follows the format

Sincerely,

Harvey Wattle

Harvey Wattle
Author/Entertainment Committee Chairperson

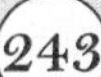

Manners Matter

As often as we use e-mail to communicate in writing, there are times when only a personal snail mail letter will do. These communications can be classified as *social notes* because they cement social relationships. Let's start with the basics of good manners, the thank-you note.

So Cousin Guido gives you a nice check for your wedding. No, you cannot endorse the back and scribble "Thank you, Guido, for the big check." Their check is not their receipt. You must write a real thank-you note. If you are a man, you cannot leave this task for your little woman. If you are the little woman, you cannot leave this task for your old man. Even if you detest the gift and the giver is a cheapskate, a thank-you must be sent . . . and it must be sent by you. Fortunately, it's nice to be nice to the nice.

Show and Tell

Thank-you notes are equally important in a business setting. Send a thank-you note for an interview, even if it didn't go especially well. The note shows that you have manners, can write clearly, and play well with others. It also allows you the opportunity to correct any misunderstandings that occurred during the interview and reiterate your strong points. Although personal thank-you notes must be handwritten, business thank-you notes can be e-mailed.

Thanks to You . . .

In addition to acknowledging someone's thoughtfulness and generosity, a thank-you note can prevent misunderstandings, such as a misrouted gift, that can set off a family feud.

When you write a thank-you note, try to . . .

- Mention the specific gift or act of kindness.
- Explain why the gift or action was appreciated.
- Make the note individualized to each person.
- Be polite and gracious, even if the gift stinks.
- Write promptly, within a few days.
- Handwrite the note on personal stationery or note cards. If your writing is poor, you can print.

A Model Thank-You Note

Use the following thank-you note as a model when you write your own:

Dear Mr. and Mrs. Jones,
Thank you for attending our wedding. Your presence made our special day even more meaningful and we are glad that we had a chance to catch up on old times. We are delighted to hear that Barbara is doing so well in the WWF and we will be sure to watch her on TV. Who would have thought that little Barbara would grow up to be BamBam the Boulder!
Thank you also for your thoughtful gift. You know that we collect antique bowling balls and this one certainly is a beauty. It will make an admirable addition to our collection.

Fondly,
Nick and Nora

S

T

U

V

W